Practice is a Dirty Word

Published by

WORDS & Music

PO Box 422, The Gap Q 4061 Australia

Ph: 07 3300 2286. www.ruthbonetti.com

First published 2002

Reprinted 2003, 2004, 2005, 2006, 2007, 2009

Cover design: Peter Fenoglio
Illustrations: John Harrison
Editing and pre-press: Bob Johnson

ISBN: 978-0-9578861-5-5

Also by Ruth Bonetti

Confident Music Performance (Words and Music)

Practice WAS a Dirty Word: Music Journal (Words and Music)

Don't Freak Out – Speak Out (Words and Music)
as Book, audio CD and e-book

Enjoy Playing the Clarinet (Oxford University Press)

Enjoy Playing the Clarinet Piano Accompaniments

Clarinet Series 2 (AMEB Grades 1-4, Allans Publishing)

Practice is a Dirty Word

How To Clean Up Your Act

Ruth Bonetti
B.Mus., M.Mus., A.R.C.M., A.Mus.A.

*Let's challenge the word 'practice'
and find ways to smarten our act!*

Foreword

I have had the pleasure of working with Ruth Bonetti for two summers in an intense music camp setting. Ruth helps students perform their best. She works beyond purely musical means by helping students address the issues that get in the way of performing their best – stage fright and lack of preparation. Ruth focuses on success for each person at every level and age group. Instead of focusing on "perfection" and the things that can never be achieved, Ruth helps students identify achievable goals.

Ruth's book on practice follows this philosophy beautifully. Page one sets the tone and hooks the reader when Ruth explodes the myth that "practice makes perfect". She never suggests that we should not strive to be our best. Rather, she helps identify a successful road towards that goal. The book is engaging and easy to read. And it is short enough that it can be read in time to get back to practising. I would strongly recommend the book for anyone, especially those for whom the fun has disappeared from "playing" music.

Jeffrey Scott Doebler, Ph.D.,
Director of Music Education and Bands,
Valparaiso University, Indiana, USA.
President, Indiana Music Educators Association

Acknowledgements

Thank you to my students over the past years, from whom I learned much, and to the many musicians, teachers and parents who have helped with comments, feedback, information and by reading the manuscript.

Thank you to my husband Antoni, for his input, encouragement and support. Thank you, André, for supplying just the right expression for the cover photograph. And Paul-Antoni, who showed that his years of practice were worthwhile by helping me develop aspects of Chapter 5.

Many thanks to my "dream team" of Peter Fenoglio (cover design), John Harrison for his so apt illustrations. How can I adequately thank my editor, Bob Johnson, who excelled himself by learning the basics of music in the interests of absolute clarity, who built up the graphics painstakingly, and who has given his time and expertise so willingly, patiently and unstintingly.

Introduction

"Go do your practice!" is the plaint of many a parent and the words music students loathe to hear. Most young musicians have an allergy to the very word "Practice". Teachers and parents struggle to entice, cajole, bribe, threaten, bully and push them into regular, committed work.

It gets worse. "Have you done your full half-hour?" Once you have zapped through the pieces once, faced a dreaded scale or two (perhaps not) – then what do you do?

The problem is that a majority of young players, even up to University levels, simply do not know how to use their practice time to achieve results. They resort to aimless ramblings which do more damage than benefit as they embed mistakes solidly into their technical foundation. It reaches the point where many players merely make noise to keep the adults off their backs.

Practice is a Dirty Word rescues you from the bogey of practice. It encourages you to "work smart", to achieve results, but within realistic time constraints. For we all have to get a life! It helps you to face and solve problems.

At last, you can face the music – by practice, which will become less of a dirty word. And as a result, you can unearth richer potential than you imagined possible. You can even surprise yourself by enjoying your practice times and the exceptional performance results which will follow.

Your music will shine.

Dedication

For my boys André, Simeon and Paul-Antoni, who have been good models for developing the topic of practice ... and have taught me much along the way.

Contents

If I were a dictator, I would eliminate the word "practice" from the vocabulary, for it becomes a bogey, a nightmare …
I would ask: "Have you already made and enjoyed music today? If not – go and make music".

Pianist, Artur Schnabel

Chapter 1

Why practice is a dirty word

Of course we all dislike practice. Unless we have a burning, exciting goal, something that carries us along.

Pianist Jorge Bolet said: "I have to be honest. I hate practising. I've always disliked it. But it's a necessity. I have to do it because I love to play."

If practice consists of making noise, rather than music, it's no wonder most players think it's a dirty word. Beethoven ridiculed the acrobats of the keyboard who "prance up and down, putsch, putsch, putsch – what does that mean? Nothing."

Does practice really make perfect?

Let me explode a myth.

Practice does not make perfect.

Not exactly. Not always. Hey, not ever. Let's face it, we can't be perfect.

Even top performers cannot be perfect. None of us can be a hundred percent perfect. Trying to be so is the biggest single cause of nerves, insecurity, depression, low self-esteem. These can cause even the most capable and talented people to give up.

The whole problem is that "practice makes perfect" has been garbled and used as a whip around our ears. Who coined that phrase, anyway? No one admits to it, but the closest we can get to its origin is that the ancient Greek philosopher Periander said: "Practice is everything." And in the 1st century BC, Roman Publilius Syrus said: "Practice is the best of instructors." Both of these are much better ways of facing practice.

On the issue of perfection and practice, the American concert pianist André Watts said: "I don't think that practising 10 hours a day has anything to do with perfection. It has more to do with being virtuous. Because truly careful practice cannot be sustained for that kind of a stretch. It becomes rote – it's like doing callisthenics. And at a certain point in your life all those extra hours are not going to improve your technique."

"Faultily faultless, icily regular, splendidly null. Dead perfection, no more," was the succinct judgement of the 19th century English poet Alfred Lord Tennyson.

His contemporary Matthew Arnold was a bit more cerebral: "Not a having and a resting, but a growing and a becoming is the character of perfection as culture conceives it."

Logan Pearsall Smith (1865–1946) took another view of perfection. He said: "The indefatigable pursuit of an unattainable perfection, even though it consists in nothing more than in the

pounding of an old piano, is what alone gives a meaning to our life on this unavailing star."

But the English novelist W. Somerset Maugham summed it up nicely: "Perfection has one grave defect; it is apt to be dull."

Don't try to play perfectly

Let us try another angle:

Intelligent thinking practice may make near-perfect.

So what is practice?

Look on it as an opportunity to:

- PLAY WITH BEAUTIFUL SOUNDS
- ENJOY THE MUSIC YOU ARE MAKING
- IMPROVE TRICKY BITS
- PLAY REGULARLY
- ZOOM FASTER AROUND THE INSTRUMENT
- AIM FOR EXCELLENCE
- EXPLORE YOUR POTENTIAL
- INCREASE YOUR BRAIN POWER (see Chapter 9)
- GIVE YOUR ABILITY WINGS
- DARE TO SUCCEED

We all enjoy the creative and communicative aspects of music more than the boring hard work. We will always find something more interesting to play than the tricky passage that really needs attention. We prefer to reassure ourselves by practising the phrases we can manage rather than face the ones we can't. How difficult it is to boycott the word "practice"! There are too few pleasant substitutes.

As long as we stay in this comfort zone, we will never discover our full potential.

Why practise?

It's all cause and effect. We reap what we sow. Especially when it comes to a concert or competition. If we know, submerged deep down under the distractions, procrastinations, avoidances, excuses and trivia, that we have not worked, who's surprised if we stuff up? It's as likely as Monday following Sunday. We deserve to be nervous. However, here's the good news!

There's a good chance we will even enjoy performing if we prepare intelligently and regularly in the months before – using our brains. We may even shrug off the butterflies and nervous greeblies. As long as we program our brains for success.

Think of your practice as computer programming. We feed in correct information about hand positions, the sequence and length of notes. Then, if a wave of panic washes over us early in a performance, it need not dump us. We can surf on automatic for a few moments, knowing that our brain will send messages to our fingers or lips without our consciously driving them. How's that for a confidence trick! (See Chapter 3 for more on this.)

Excuses, excuses...

My blood sugar dropped, so I just had to take a rest

The downside is ... computer viruses

We can crash if viruses are programmed into the learning stages; perhaps we hurriedly punched mistakes or clumsy fingerings into a passage. These will surface when we try to deliver under stress. The whole secret is in creating a good program ... call it practice if you like.

Under pressure, your brain remembers the murky fog it felt every time it approached those mean triplets ... which are actually only F# minor, if you look closely. If you work at that scale away from your concerto, you can rattle off its busy passages with such flashy fingers that you'll feel waves of red-hot envy blast from the other guys. Better still, you will approach the music with that fresh, relaxed attitude so necessary to play Mozart well. You can throw off the difficult passages as if they are a cinch.

So, why waste time practising scales?

Look at the score of your favourite Mozart, Bach or Vivaldi movement. You will see it is a mix of, yes, scales and arpeggios, dominant 7th chords, some scales with detours and sequences. If you establish a strong foundation by practising your scales and related chords you will fast track to fluency in playing your concertos.

If you practise scales only as they occur within your piece, you will find yourself stumbling. As you note more and more of your mistakes on your music it becomes so splattered with pencilled arrows, circles, sharps and flats that you become discouraged at the sight of it.

Is practice such a dirty word?

Sure, it is. Who's pretending? Okay, so you're normal. Very few performers actually like practice. But only losers give up easily. Winners persevere – and see top results. Let's discover why it is so hard to face.

- **You have to work alone, motivate yourself.**

Unlike sports, where team spirit spurs you on.

Cures: Aim to get a musical life. Improve fast so you can join a band or orchestra soon.

Memo: Instead of grouching at well-meaning parents who want to sit in with you sometimes, turn their zeal to good purpose – as cheer-leaders at your next recital. They will deliver less routine aggro when they are given a channel for their energy.

- **Beginners can't read the squiggly notes.**

Music is just another language. Do you remember your first year at school when you stumbled slowly through "easy-peasy" books? Now you read automatically, without thinking. If you persevere, the language of music will become just as fluent.

Cures: When you are given the new piece, pencil the names underneath the notes. Say or sing them aloud as you finger. After a few weeks you won't need this prop.

Photocopy and enlarge each note onto flash cards. Call out the names and play them, shuffle the cards to random order, play again.

Memo: The sooner you tackle the reading issue the sooner you can make real progress. Just do it.

- **You don't know how to put your time to good use.**

Parents and teachers nag: "You must practise for half an hour each day!" Like; what do you do once you've played it all through once? Perhaps they just don't realise how clever you are, that you have it all done so soon. However, they may judge you by their other students. Many players zoom through a piece like a pin-ball game; brrrm brrm kerplunk zoom splat keep going zoom. They crash through the same mistakes every time, digging them deeper into their memory pit.

Cure: Ask your teacher to map out a daily balanced work-out. For example:

- warm-ups, finger movers
- tone growth
- exercises, pieces and sight reading
- fun pieces to end with.

• **You don't see the results of your work.**

So, you did prepare all week, regularly, busily. You feel cheated because the next lesson is a bummer.

Cure: Hold in there. Often it takes a few days or even weeks for the effect of that hard work to show. The lesson after will probably show top results. Your teacher will send you home laden with new pieces.

• **You can't reach those goals way off on the horizon.**

Cure: Set yourself short-term goals. Like: In these 15 minutes I will learn F# minor. Or: I have five minutes to memorise bar 10.

• **Often practice seems like a bottomless pit.**

Cures: Start a scrap book of your certificates, exam reports, press-clippings. Browse through to boost self-esteem on the days when improvement seems minuscule.

Perhaps you have set only long-term goals. Ask your teacher to organise a short or medium-term challenge, perhaps a low-key concert or competition. Although...

- **If you're worried about a concert or exam, this may increase your reluctance.**

Cure: Prepare! So many people can't be wrong! A wide cross-section of musicians were asked "What helps you cope with performance nerves?" Almost all answered "Preparation!" (See Chapter 8)

Why should we practise?

Scientific studies show young musicians increase their brain power by regular playing of music. Applying this increased brain power to practice will lead to better and more confident presentation. How results of practice – or lack of it – can affect performance are shown in the following examples.

Scenario 1: The story of Brad Bravado. Our hero has to play a new piece at the end-of-term concert in a month. He skims through the notes – nothing too mean there. A few tricky bits, but ... they fell into place after a couple of restarts. It's quite a long blow but, hey, "it'll be right on the night". Come the night. He's not used to playing straight through without stopping. It was a very long blow! Ran out of puff halfway. And those rotten passages fell apart. Couldn't go back to fix them ... he did forget and have a second go once, and of course the accompanist got all flustered. Didn't realise the tempi would need to go so fast. At that speed, passages which look easy are downright evil. Afterwards, rushed off-stage in a real state.

Scenario 2: Meet Ms Goody Try-Hard. Started learning that new piece for the concert two months ago. Planned out the tempo and earmarked the tricky passages. Tickled those every day, just a few minutes, slowly. Put on the metronome, dead slow, in quaver beats. Aimed to move a notch faster every day. Started rehearsing with the pianist a few weeks before. Pencilled in cues, listened to recordings. Nicely organised on the day. Backstage, relaxed with deep breaths, stretching. Overall, the concert sailed along smoothly.

An old saying goes: "The amateur practises until he can get it right, the professional until he can't get it wrong." But we need to know how to practise. If we reinforce mistakes instead of the correct notes, we're wasting time. As many are. Might as well watch TV.

Hold it! Instead of changing channels, turn the page to learn how you can get good results in half the time.

Chapter 2

Okay, so how much practice?

Many players kill time by making mindless noise while clock watching. They focus on asking how many minutes or hours they should practise, rather than the positive results they hope to achieve. It is more constructive to consider the positive outcomes and goals you want to attain.

Get real. Maybe you spent an hour with your hands on or near your instrument, but only 10 minutes of this time achieved any progress.

How many of these time stealers do you admit to?

Classic time wasters:

- **Improvise the ultimate Chopsticks variation**
- **Play the easy bits at double speed**
- **Adjust the music stand**
- **File fingernails, check posture in mirror, change hairstyle**
- **Play computer games**
- **Play last exam's pieces twice as fast**
- **Browse through XYZ in music dictionary**
- **Erase all fingerings from last year's recital music**

Before you decide to try any of these or the dozens of other time-wasters, remember that parents and teachers are wise to them. Such time-fillers are all very well if you're happy with zero progress.

Use your time to get better, not worse

If your work is brainless, because you wish you were elsewhere (like on the computer) you will play like a robot. Expect automatic, robotic results.

And you will feed in mistakes, mistakes which will come out in performance.

Look on practice as a journey. You're driving towards a destination. You haven't got one? Then set one. Anything. An exam? A recital? To finish the grade book and start another?

Your teacher gives directions and weekly updates to your map (in the practice notebook) which will see you arrive at your destination eventually. You can also add your own detours and shortcuts. After all, you're at the wheel.

And if you choose to drive over bumpy, unsealed tracks, littered with potholes and rocks, your vehicle will suffer worse wear and tear. It's all the more streetwise to choose a direct route, or a better road, so your journey is smooth, relatively enjoyable and you arrive fresh and positive. So your impressions are not dusty, tired and frazzled. How long the journey takes is largely your decision.

You can make it an easy ride by following a few simple, clear signposts. Listen to directives like "Use the third finger here" or "Put the thumb on this note and the others will fall into place."

Find the important linchpin. Like, if I drive slower on an unfamiliar route, I am less likely to get lost. Don't speed!

Drive with a clear head, not bogged down with aggro because some adult made you travel this way. Or because you'd rather stay home and watch TV.

Visualise yourself arriving at your destination. Look forward, not back longingly at the safety of the couch and the remote control. That's couch potato stuff.

Be an action man or action woman. Get in there and make results happen. Choose success.

How to work smart

Ask not: How much practice, but

How much do I hope to achieve today?

____

____

____

How to plan your practice time

It helps if you and your teacher spend a few minutes together at the first lesson, discussing mutual goals for progress. In the front of your practice note-book, set out three columns for short-term, medium and long-term goals. Leave a space for a satisfying tick or sticker as you achieve each level. Review these aims each term or semester.

Short-term goals	Medium	Long

With these expectations set out clearly, both you and your teacher can focus on steady progress to meet them.

Every player has different abilities, aspirations and conflicting activities. Most teenage players with average self-expectations find teachers are satisfied if they aim for at least a half-hour's practice per day. With your goals in place, you may find yourself increasing the time of your own accord.

Discuss with your teacher what progress is reasonable for your situation and standard.

Surely you want to keep turning pages to new pieces, rather than sit on the same boring ones all year? Which usually means they will

worsen instead of improve as staleness bogs you down. You begin to see why practice became a dirty word?

Decide how often you should have new material

Each week? Fortnight? Month? If monthly, what about a short, easy new etude each week?

How much regular practice would your teacher expect in order to achieve such momentum?

What foundation work would enable you to manage this new work?

A relevant scale and arpeggio? A study which reinforces similar problems?

It's no surprise that many students suffer from allergies to grossly boring technical studies. The sad truth is that the musical worth of many "studies" is painfully and pitifully slim. Be warned, however. You will need to use good psychology and negotiation skills to avoid them. For if you complain and ridicule studies on such grounds it will seem a mere cop-out unless particularly well-reasoned.

A "wallpaper" etude might recycle the same issues and patterns for two pages. Prepare it industriously for a few weeks. Then, when your teacher is suitably softened with your positive effort, negotiate. Offer to learn another study which reinforces the same challenge but in a contrasting style.

Most teachers will respond positively to such enterprise. It will be worth it just to see their expression! Because you showed yourself as a discerning player, your teacher should get the message and choose technical etudes which have some musical value and blacklist those which seem to be set for the sole purpose of keeping kids off the streets.

Perhaps there are few worthwhile etudes available for your particular instrument? You may be just the person to compose something interesting which addresses particular technical aspects.

Set the goal posts

Successful players set clear goals to keep themselves motivated. This way, we take charge of our lives rather than let life take charge of us. But sometimes we aim too high, miss and give up.

Break large goals into smaller, bite-sized parts. Map out lists of short-term, medium and long-term goals. Relish the satisfaction of crossing them off as they are achieved. Sit down with your notebook well before the next big event, to map out a program, listing the technical and musical challenges this involves.

For example:

Two days	*Clap rhythms. Learn the triplets, page 5.*
One week	*Sight read whole movement, slow and correct. Sing, think through dynamics. Memorise page 1.*
One month	*Learn whole movement, at a comfortable speed, memorised.*
Three months	*Perform whole movement up to speed.*
Eight months	*Learn entire concerto.*

Encourage yourself by keeping a journal or practice notebook. As well as planning time usage in advance, you can look back later and relish your improvement. Copy in tricky passages to occupy spare moments and as backstage warm-ups.

Better regular than binge

A steady, regular practice regimen is far more effective than doing it in fits and starts. Work smart so you build each day's progress a notch higher rather than scramble it together the night before your lesson. Haphazard practice runs the risk of overstrained hands and fingers, sore lips (if you are a wind or brass player) or laryngitis (if you are a singer).

At the beginning of a practice work-out, ask yourself what is the most important aspect needing your time, energy and work.

When to practise?

A quick-fix answer is: The same time is the best time.

Establish a routine of always practising, say, before breakfast or after dinner, whatever suits your schedule. This pattern can carry you through the pain threshold of having to resist other time guzzlers like TV or the Internet. Mornings have the advantage that you are fresh, your brain is alert.

Hot tip!

Any practice done immediately after your lesson, no matter how short, is time well spent, for you can consolidate new ideas and material while they are fresh in your mind.

Reality check

Many people find their life is busy busy busy. Just keeping up with all those extra activities is a big juggling act. So you'll have to PLAN SMART.

Jot down your activities against the days of the week. Plan ahead with a schedule allotting time for practice along these lines:

Day	Other activities	Practice
Monday	*Basketball, lots of homework*	*25 minutes*
Tuesday	*After-school care, late home*	*20 min morning* *15 min evening*
Wednesday	*Music lesson tomorrow, no sport*	*45 minutes*
Thursday	*Lesson after soccer practice*	*25 min morning* *10 min evening*
Friday	*Heavy day; tests, soccer, ballet*	*No practice*
Saturday	*Soccer game, work at Pizza Hut*	*Aim for 20-30 minutes*
Sunday	*Sport, movies, recreation*	*Catch up what fell short during the week, plus some fun sight-reading or duets.*

Set goals for each block of practice time

You have 45 minutes available. Make up a work chart something like this:

Minutes	*Goal*	*Material*
5	*Warm-up, develop tone*	*Long sustained notes, slow scales*
5	*Finger warm-up*	*Faster scales, arpeggios*
5	*Learn triplets*	*Sonata Page 3 (Say aloud while fingering. Slow work)*
10	*Consolidate, apply*	*Similar triplets in Whoosit study*
5	*Relaxation*	*A drink of water, deep breathing and stretching, chasing the dog in the garden*
5	*Learn chromatics bars 1-6*	*Chromatic scales. Whatsit etude*
5	*Apply*	*Similar fingerings in Mozart sonata*
5	*Revise triplet passage*	*Sight-read a triplet piece*

Set yourself achievable, reasonable, short-term aims each day. Within each time slot, allow yourself several minutes' relaxation, movement, a breath of fresh air, a drink of water. Oxygen and water are powerful brain foods. You will then use work-time more efficiently and minimise risk of repetitive strain injury. Give yourself the satisfaction of crossing goals off the list when they are reached. Reward yourself with a pat on the back or a treat.

Don't give up at the first hurdle

To climb a mountain, we have to plod through valleys and cross boring flat plateaus before we reach the heights and enjoy the view from the summit. There are also times when we would far prefer sport or just hanging out. We've all got to have a life!

How to survive busy times

There are times, like the last year at high school, when, unless you're aiming for a tertiary music course, your basic studies inevitably must take priority. Warn your music teacher when a pressured phase looms on the horizon, like final year test blocks. An enterprising teacher can find other ways to use the lesson constructively, giving a mix of general knowledge, aural tests, sight-reading, theory. Or listen to recordings, talk about the background and historical framework of the composers, hear the gossip about composers' lives. (Don't believe that music lessons must be deadly serious!) You may discover that instead of dreading the lessons because "I haven't practised" you may look forward to them as a relief from other school pressures.

For wind and brass players, uncomfortable times when orthodontic braces have been tightened can be eased with similar tactics, especially talking through the music.

> **R.I.P.**
>
> Alessandro Stradella eloped with a lady whose lover had him assassinated.
>
> A jealous rival murdered violin virtuoso Jean-Marie Leclair on the steps of his Paris home.
>
> Ernst Chausson died after crashing his bicycle in 1899.
>
> Johann Schobart and his family died after mistaking toadstools for mushrooms.

In such difficult times ask yourself:

- Where am I aiming?
- What do I want from my music?

Recreation? Light relief? A bit of fun? Social

life? Progress? Achieve ...? Challenge/ consolidate/ mark time?

- **Do I hope to maintain last year's levels, to grow, or just to mark time?**

Tip off your teacher about your workload. He or she can then select – as much as possible – music you will enjoy without being too stretched. It is far better to tread water for a while than be washed down the drain by waves of overwork and choke on a lather of guilt. If you pull the plug too readily you may regret it later and wish you'd stayed in the swim.

The clue to survival of such pressured times is to keep your teacher on side by being open and up-front. Together, set some interesting short-term goals, like a relaxed student concert or competition so that memories of your long lost past successes are not merely depressing. Keep some embers alive, so that sparks can revive later when you have more time and puff.

But practice wrecks my social life!

That's easily fixed: turn it into social life. Play duets and trios or improvise with friends. Include sight-reading and, if relevant, transposition practice. Join a youth orchestra or band. Form your own band, do gigs. Even if you have no intention of turning pro, it can be profitable to reach your highest possible standard. Many tertiary students earn far higher rates by teaching or gigging than they would working in a supermarket or hamburger joint. Triple or quadruple!

Where to practise

Pianists are more restricted than singers or other instrumentalists, who can practise almost anywhere. Most institutions have a chronic shortage of studios. In my own university days, I practised my clarinet in the lift, usually at night when there were fewer people to distract me ... and vice versa (try scales ascending and descending with the movement), in broom cupboards, the college pantry, an engineering lab, in the bathroom (flattering acoustics) and on a train (largely inaudible).

Anywhere is suitable as long as you have:

- Space to make noise

  Grumbling family members or neighbours inhibit you from playing out with your richest sound. Such situations require initiative, negotiating skills and lateral thinking. Perhaps you could organise to use an empty church hall or school classroom.
- Space by yourself

  You must feel free to actually work at passages. If someone else is in the room, even your best supporter, you will not really practise; rather, you will feel pressured to perform. Which is not the same thing.
- Good posture
- Enough area to move freely

  Practice performed in a cramped coat-hanger shape posture will do more harm than good.

A standing position is ideal for working as it encourages an upright posture. (Small spaces like the pantry may just be okay.) If you do sit, you will need a chair which has good back support to help you resist slouching tendencies. However, sitting on a stool can be a good solution as there is no tempting back to lean against.

An adjustable music stand is essential. If you try to prop music haphazardly at an uncomfortable height or on your bed, your posture will suffer.

The Big No-No:

Never practise on your bed. It is too tempting!

Is it possible to over-practise?

Parents and teachers may seem to push the line that practising for endless hours must do endless good. As long as they hear noise coming from the room, they're happy. Right? (Until they come in and see your iPod earphones.)

Certainly, many gifted children practise long hours because they genuinely enjoy the satisfaction of challenges met, progress achieved. Some obsessive personalities feel a need to practise until they drop. If this is through genuine enjoyment and satisfaction, so be it. Avoid guilt-tripping. Long hours' practising are not a virtue unless you prove something in them. True, you do not want to run the risk of repetitive strain injury, which may set you back totally.

Pianist, composer and conductor Robert Schumann spoke from experience when he said "It is very foolish to devote hours each day to mere mechanical practice in which neither head nor heart are concerned."

In his *Advice to Young Musicians*, he wrote: "You must practise scales and other finger exercises assiduously. There are, however, many people who fancy they attain perfection by spending, even until an advanced age, several hours daily in mechanical execution; that is as if a person should exert himself to repeat his ABC faster and faster. Employ your time better."

As a young student, he wrote in his diary: "Overdone technical studies. Laming of my right hand." To be fair, it is likely that this was caused when Schumann tried to get clever by inventing a mechanical gadget to improve his finger independence.

Polish composer Frederic Chopin recommended no more than three hours' practice a day. The respected violin teacher Carl Flesch ridiculed exaggerated mechanical repetition which "develops either intelligent bunglers or brainless acrobats" at the risk of artistic, physical and spiritual ruin.

Donald Westlake, for decades the principal clarinettist of the Sydney Symphony Orchestra, learned balance:

"My own view after a lifetime of over-practice is this: there's a great blue ocean out there, for swimming, fishing and sailing … If you have to do more than, say, three hours' practice a day, even in your formative years, maybe, just maybe, you're looking in the wrong direction!"

It is reasonable that if your year's work is consistent, intelligent and has seen progress through good time management, then you deserve a break. If you practise five, preferably six days a week, then take a day's rest without guilt trips. A few weeks' complete break away from the instrument each year can be refreshing. Before your holiday, ask your teacher for a system of recuperation exercises as there will inevitably be lost tone and fluency when you blow the dust off the instrument. Enjoy your break!

Chapter 3

How to work smart

"What you think is what you shall find," said the Greek philosopher Aristotle. And the American guru of presentation Norman Vincent Peale said: "You are not what you think you are – but what you think, you are."

Focus your mind on success. Practice is simply a matter of programming your mind. Think of each new piece or page of music as a blank CD. Whatever is burned on to it is imprinted indelibly. It is important to set a positive, clear first impression.

How to program your brain for success

Begin by clearing your mind of untidy clutter. Ban negative put-downs.

Bite your tongue on words like "I can't" – or you won't.

Turn down the volume on the little voices in your head who nag: "Bet you make a fool of yourself."

If you say "I'll probably stuff it up" – then you will. "I always mess this up" – you will continue to do so. "I will never get this even" – nor will you, until you change to "**I CAN!**"

See yourself succeeding – and you probably will.

WITH STEADY THINKING, REGULAR PRACTICE AND POSITIVE SELF-TALK YOU CAN DO IT!

The point is not how much you practise, but how much you hope to achieve.

Many students "work hard" but achieve little because they play without thinking. Or they waste time practising what they can play easily and avoid the hard bits. They stay in the comfort zone of what they can do rather than face the challenge of what they can't.

"You must do the thing you think you cannot do" – Eleanor Roosevelt, former American First Lady.

> **Hot tip!**
>
> *PRACTISE WHAT YOU CAN'T PLAY, INSTEAD OF WHAT YOU CAN*

Instead of working hard at what you can already handle well, you need to manage your time and "work smart" at what you find difficult.

If you plan your time and set your goals intelligently and constructively, you will develop a momentum that will move you through the drudgery of short and medium term legwork to realise your satisfying long-term dreams.

A clear mind makes successful performance

• *Set Positive Rather than Negative Memories*

Brain space is wasted when we allow the misty memories of failure to fog up our minds. Every time we play, speak or sing a passage incorrectly, we cover over our impression of it with another murky memory of failure. We should aim to use practice time to build a solid basis of memories of success. For surely, when we approach that particular passage in a performance situation, our brain will recall the strongest impression.

• *First Impressions Count!*

Your memory will retain first impressions clearest so it is important that these are accurate. Most people remember best that information which is taken through their eyes. ("Average" people retain about 80% of information through their eyes, 12% aurally.) Next day, your brain only has to remember, not re-learn. From now on, practice is a relatively simple process of consolidation.

Even sight-readable, simple pieces benefit from a clear first reading. It is far easier to pull out weeds (or wrong notes) when they are spindly, before they grow tough trunks. Create the habit of "play it right" rather than of "play it wrong", otherwise known as hit'n'miss.

Double your results in half the time

Think back over recent practice. How much of that was spent un-learning mistakes and re-learning the correct notes? Yet if you learn a passage accurately the first time, your practice in the following days will consist merely of reinforcing and consolidating, rather than wasting time by correcting mistakes. With this approach you will soon realise that you can increase your learning pace significantly and cover much more material in less time.

How to work smart to learn a new piece

Your goal is to create positive, correct habits; of a pattern, a note sequence, a rhythm or a physical position (of hand, arm or embouchure). If your habit is clear and secure, then when you perform under pressure you can safely go into auto-drive. Without conscious thought, your subconscious reproduces that habit. So make sure all your habits are correct ones!

> **Hot tip!**
>
> *PRACTICE MAKES PERMANENT RATHER THAN PERFECT*

It has been said that if the average person repeats an action 50 times, it becomes a habit. For a high-school science class experiment, a boy decided to tie his shoelaces in a new way. After repeating it 50 times, he automatically tied his laces this way from then on.

Vary the practice of your new piece with some of these different approaches:

- **Without your instrument**, begin by looking through new music as if reading a book. Note issues that may need attention, sing through tricky rhythms, preferably using Solfa.

- **Analyse** what structures and patterns are in the music, e.g scales, arpeggios, chromatics, repetitions, dominant 7th chords – all of which are in the line below.

A piece bristling with accidentals (like the excerpt from *The Flight of the Bumble Bee* below) may be as simple as the chromatic scales you have already practised.

- **Say aloud and finger the notes.** Play the notes in equal time – without rhythm. Then play the rhythm on bongo drums (or on empty ice-cream containers). Join rhythm and notes together.
- **Play out-of-time.** Don't move from one note or chord until absolutely sure of the next.
- **The Add-a-Bit Method:** Isolate the tricky passage. Start with a manageable few notes. Add a block of notes, then progress with further segments.

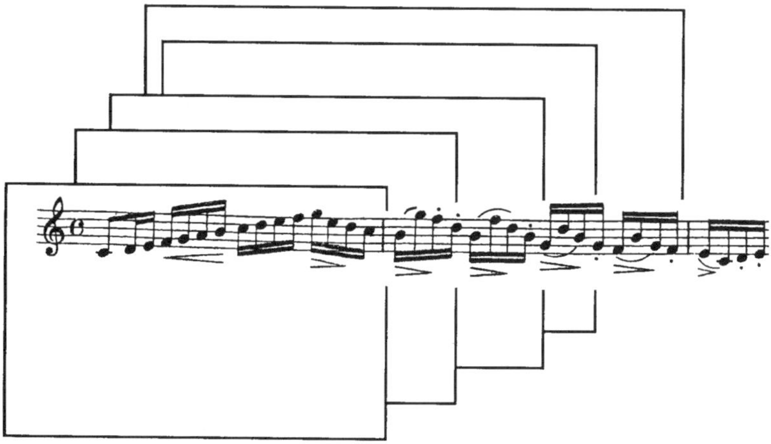

- **The Building-Block Method:** Did you enjoy playing Lego? To learn a new piece, work in small units like building bricks as shown in the illustration below. First, bar 1, over and over until it is secure. Now, bar 2. Join bars 1 and 2 together, by playing them together, paying especial attention to the few notes which join them. Next, practise bar 3, and then cement it to bar 2.

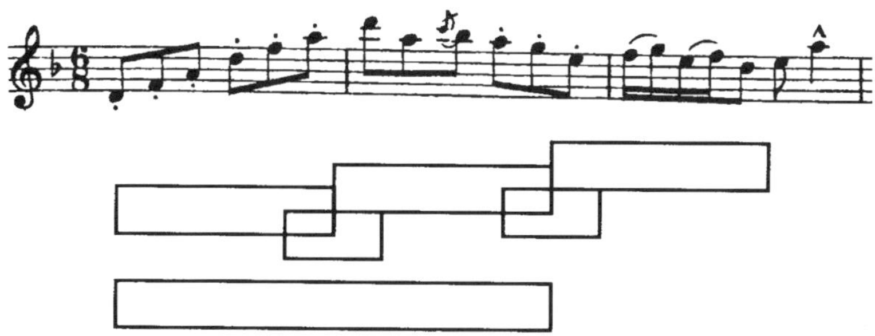

Discover if your brain can successfully remember all the material learned thus far. By challenging it with short segments it can keep up with any demands. So often we practice in huge chunks, reading through whole pages rather than breaking it down to brick-sized bits.

- **Rhythm of the Waves Method:** By working in small units, the brain can concentrate – relax – concentrate – relax. Just as the waves ebb and flow, while progressively drawing further out to sea, so our technique can be stretched, then relaxed, in order to challenge further until soon the whole page is mastered.
- **The Expanding Ripples Method:** This is similar to the above. You have a tricky passage. Analyse the difficult area. Mark the problem few notes with a pencilled slur under them and play them. Repeat these until you can play them four or five times without a mistake. Then add the next note or two (widening the circle of ripples). Repeat this process until you can play the problem passage correctly so it is clear and the ripples hold the passage together as illustrated below.

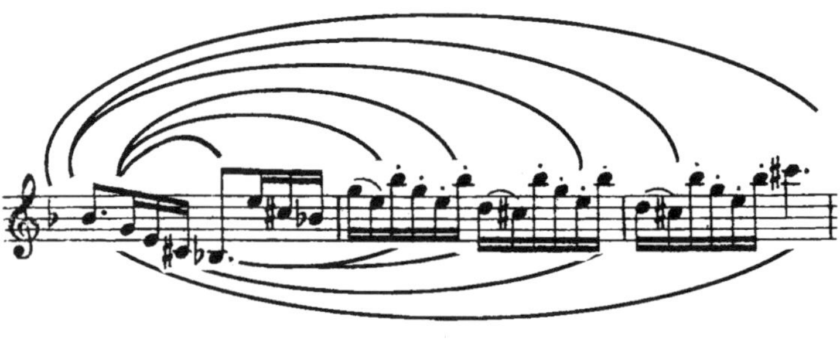

Speed kills music

Mozart wrote: "It is much easier to play a thing quickly than to play it slowly."

Why? Because at top speed, we don't have time to notice or face the subtle challenges.

During the early stages of tackling a new work, most of the playing should be at a slow tempo, as comfortable and rhythmic as Grandma's rocking chair. Zipping through the score while dragging fingers and brain behind causes tensions, missed connections, confusions.

Start at half-speed. "Ohhhh," you mutter, "boring, yawn, yawn!" But look at your relaxed fingers!

Notice how those mean passages become feasible, how rhythms seem less complicated, how your brain has time to sequence patterns out of chaos.

Walk before you run

To see progress, practise with a metronome, each day moving one or two notches faster, so your fingers and brain don't even notice any increase in speed. After a few weeks, with the tempo even faster than that needed in performance, there is room for relaxation. Now you can play fast and fluently, with a minimum of tension.

Put to the test

I first realised just how effective is this method when preparing the Weber Concertino to be performed with a Swedish orchestra, conducted by my husband, Antoni. After weeks of slow practice, I felt quite comfortable with the performance, which ended with a suitably flashy, rousing finale. After the performance, Toni whistled: "Phew! That last page really zapped along! The orchestra could barely keep up." "Fast?" I asked. "It was just a comfortable Allegro." I listened to the tape. "You're right, it is fast. I never knew my fingers could move like that!" If only I had applied such practice techniques to earlier projects!

How to tackle a tricky passage

• Isolate problem areas. Practise these daily, slowly, over and over. You practise not merely to "get it right" but to make it easy.

• Reduce a difficult passage to a few notes. Anyone can face just a few notes. Gradually enlarge.

• Parrot Fashion Works: Rote learning has had bad press in recent years, but its value is underestimated. Thoughtful – not mindless – repetition is a fast track to success.

• The 10 in a Row Snakes and Ladders Game: Play the tricky passage correctly 10 consecutive times to be fool-proof. If you slip on the ninth time, it's down the snake to start all over again.

• Pianists should practise each hand separately. Try to play one hand and sing the other part.

• Photocopy the page (enlarged), then:

a) Read or play it through slowly to analyse the problems.

b) Mark any problem areas with a felt pen, noting repeated patterns or where the direction changes.

c) Break it into smaller bricks and work as suggested above.

d) Now practise each brick with different rhythms. Turn duplets into triplets, or into dotted rhythms.

e) Divide that passage into groups of five notes: play the first five notes – stop and look at the next group of five – play them – look ahead – play five more notes. Divide the passage into groups of six notes ... then seven.

f) Play the passage with different articulation patterns and rhythms.

g) How much can you remember? Shut your eyes and play. Or place the music progressively higher so your eyes rely less on the printed page.

h) Memorise the passage. This will add security in performance.

i) Play as written, starting a few bars before the tricky notes. Consciously relax as it approaches. You managed? Great!

j) Reward yourself. Give yourself a jelly bean. Say out loud "I did it! I played it correctly!" Savour your success.

k) Repeat to prove that it was no fluke. Congratulate yourself.

Ways to jazz up practice

Variety is the spice. Keep your brain challenged and lively by setting yourself some of these different methods of practice.

- Dem Bones: Play the skeleton of a melodic line without the extra stuff – especially those written in Alberti Bass style.
- Water Music: Sing the piece through in the shower. We learn a lot from a natural process like singing – about breathing and phrasing, nuance, direction, punctuation.
- Photocopy the music: With coloured pens, highlight sequences, bits of a scale or chord, directions of phrases, which sections answer each other, or contrast.
- Photocopy the difficult passages, enlarged to A3 size: Tape your performance. Listen back and highlight any mistakes with a fluorescent pen. Analyse the weak spots, why you lost the plot. Divide crucial connections into bite-size bits and repeat them over and over. A week later repeat the process and admire the improvement

between the two pages. Give yourself a jelly bean.

- Recording session: Tape yourself and listen back, pencil and score in hand, noting errors and weak spots.
- Compare your effort with professional recordings of the piece.
- Play music with accompaniment – either with a pianist or with a taped recording.
- Switch rhythms around. Play evens as dotteds, dotteds as evens.
- Odds and sods. Play passages of duplets as triplets or quintuplets.
- Imagine colours into the music. A dark, deep purple on *mezzo forte* low notes, a brilliant red *fortissimo* upper register, a rich green like the grass after heavy rain for a *cantabile* passage. Add a sliver of light to contrast.
- Turn rhythmic hassles into aerobic exercises by moving as you play or sing. Studies show that physical movement helps our brains absorb information

FYI

Photocopying music is acceptable if you own a printed copy of the music. Many students, teachers and parents routinely photocopy whole works of music. This saving of money is short sighted as publishers cannot afford to print further repertoire. The music may become unavailable if they cannot reprint. Many publishers struggle, even go out of business. Photocopying is a form of stealing. Please restrict it to the legal limits of enabling tricky page turns, of 10% of a work, or when a piece is known to be out of print.

better. Cross-Crawl, or cross-lateral walking in place, involves alternately moving one arm and the opposite leg and then the other arm and leg, such as when we march. This accesses both brain hemispheres simultaneously and is an ideal warm-up to improve coordination, breathing and stamina, and to enhance hearing, vision and learning.

- If you have a dog, take it and your music for a walk where there are few people to look strangely at you, and sing the piece through.
- March, jog, dance to your piece while you sing it through in your head.
- Invent a story line to go with a piece. A melodrama or soapie, with different voices interacting, arguing, discussing.

- Analyse the harmony, form or skeletal shape: decide which parts are important, which are subservient.
- Play window views: If that mean page looks too daunting to face, isolate a bite-size bit and cover the bars on either side with post-it notes. Play what you see in the window. Move the papers to focus on further bars.
- Play Ping Pong: Isolate two tricky passages; play one, then the other, then return to the first. As you alternate between the two your brain has to remember the challenges afresh. This works well with scales. Bounce between the harmonic and the melodic versions, then throw in the major scale for a fresh ball.
- Sit or lie comfortably. (The one time you can justify working on your bed!) Look at the music while you sing the notes and finger them.
- Tip of the iceberg: Ask yourself what is the bulk of a scale or piece of music that you can already play reasonably? What is the tip? Maybe 20% or 10% – three or four notes – need most attention, for example, in the G# melodic minor at right. Focus on the "tip of the iceberg" notes for 80% of your time. The rest plays itself.

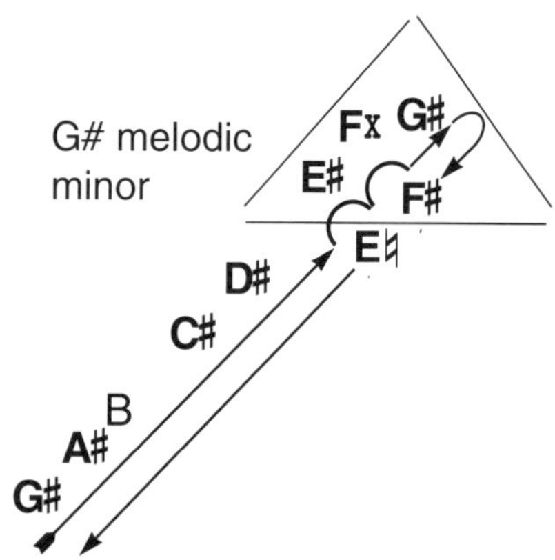

Now imagine yourself succeeding, sailing through like the greatest players. What you envisage can happen. You're on your way to success.

Chapter 4

How to fix mistakes

Often as a student I learned new music too fast, resulting in foreign notes and stumbles. I am amazed how strongly those first impressions were etched into my subconscious. Even after hours of diligent, intelligently applied rehearsal techniques, that mistake was suctioned to my mind. Playing the same piece 20 years later, even with a new, pristine copy of the music, my mind and fingers hesitate, falter, stumble, drawn irresistibly to that fault learned in a moment's careless reading. What a waste of some beautiful repertoire, pock-marked with mindless mistakes!

Like weeding, it's far easier if you pull out the little mistakes early before they grow to a tough, thorny bush. Here's how:

- Decide which is the problem (weedy) note.
- Highlight it in colour (use pencil, not felt-pen – using permanent pens on printed music is a big no-no).
- Transplant a fresh, correct note, or add "fertiliser" to a timid, unsure note. Say aloud and finger.
- Water the ground on either side by playing the note with its close neighbours slowly, five times.
- Add a few more notes, play five times consecutively.
- Gradually increase the moist area around the new "plant" with more "well watered" notes.
- Check: Go back and play the whole phrase – five times in a row. If you make a mistake on the fifth try, start over again.
- It worked? Now try it with your eyes shut.
- Again okay. Give yourself a jelly bean. (No, not three!)

Strengthen weak spots

Adapt your work patterns to suit the various situations, drawing from the following ideas.

• Play it differently. Any trick that stretches your brain is a good thing – brains work all the better for challenge. Opposition strengthens resolve.

• Analyse the problem. Is this a poor habit? A note reading weakness? A tricky note pattern? Finger stretch? Glitch in reading skills?

• Eyecatchers: If you consistently miss a note because its interval is wider than expected pencil a small mark between the two crucial notes so your eye will notice the stretch. Or if a string of sequences suddenly changes direction, a pencilled arrow can alert your eye to this.

• Play opposites, be contrary: If a passage is written *legato*, practise it detached; if *staccato,* play smoothly. Dotted rhythms can be played evenly and vice versa. If it is notated soft, play loud.

• Trapeze: If a run ascends, practise it descending and vice versa. Up and down, over and over. Note and reinforce any stumbles, for a stumble shows that you have not fully absorbed the correct passage or interval.

• Odds and evens: If a passage of notes falls into groups of four, play it in threes or in fives.

• The Metronome Crawl: Many mistakes are caused by rushing, which happens most in mean passages. While practising, cure this by slowing right down so you can think straight. From the beginning, play difficult passages at half-speed. Your fingers remain relaxed if you move the metronome just a notch or two each day. Write each new speed you achieved in your practice diary so you can enjoy your progress.

• Arrested notes: Stop on the note before the problem-case. Think how it should feel to play it before you do so.

• Backward steps: Work from the end backwards. Tackle a tricky phrase or line or piece in small backward steps. Begin at the cadence with a few notes. Add a note or two progressively until you are comfortable with the whole sequence.

• Memorise: Any insecure areas develop confidence in performance if they are memorised.

• Odd moment filler: Recall any tricky passages in your mind away from your instrument. At the same time finger the notes on whatever comes to hand as an "instrument" – a pencil can become a clarinet, a cricket bat a saxophone, a tennis racquet a violin, a desk, a piano. You don't have to make a noise to practise.

How to fix bung rhythm

Many players try to manage on "hit and miss" or "near enough" counting, or no counting at all. They fool themselves if they imagine this is not obvious to a discerning listener. An adjudicator or examiner can usually tell in the first phrase which candidates do not have a reliable system of counting.

Just "counting" is often not the issue. Accurate, reliable rhythm is not just a matter of saying or thinking "one-two-three-four" (perhaps unevenly). Those who rely on the foot-tapping method may be disappointed. Even a heavily thumping boot doesn't ensure even measures, as that foot may conveniently "wait" when a string of notes must be fitted into the beat. Erratic foot-tapping can become a problem especially when you are sitting. Worse is out-of-time thumping.

Instead, sing and march in your practice time. But most people think they would look like a dork so they flinch at the thought. Which is a pity as it's probably the quickest fix. Hey, enterprising people can turn it into aerobics and get fit at the same time. Let's put a positive spin to this idea. One day you might make good money playing in a military band.

Students also hate it when teachers ask them to clap, though that's actually another quick fix to improve confusions and irregularity. If the teacher gets you to use something cool like bongo drums, you soon learn how to play rhythms without being bothered by notes, bowings and articulations. You can improvise at home with saucepans or ice-cream containers.

True rhythm, spot-on and reliable, needs an understanding of how the beats are formed and subdivided (ask your teacher for a rerun if you're not 100% sure). One reason many students are confused by the whole rhythm thing is the use of meaningless names like quaver and crotchet. The logical system is the German-American one where whole notes are divided into half notes, quarter notes, sixteenth notes, thirty-second notes and so on. They all add up as you will see if you think in terms of money:

A whole note	𝅝	=	\$4	=	8 x 50¢	=	16 x 25¢
A half note	𝅗𝅥	=	\$2	=	4 x 50¢	=	8 x 25¢
A quarter note	♩	=	\$1	=	2 x 50¢	=	4 x 25¢
An eighth note	♪	=	50¢	=	2 x 25¢		
A sixteenth note	𝅘𝅥𝅯	=	25¢				

The table above shows that if a sixteenth note is 25¢, a whole note is \$4. But a whole note is also eight 50¢ pieces or sixteen 25¢ pieces.

So, when written as manuscript, a whole note can be shown:

This monetary comparison makes sense when you come to building common patterns. For example, if you want to play a dotted quarter note followed by an eighth note, written as manuscript:

Think of the dotted quarter note as worth \$1.50 (three 50¢) and the eighth note as 50¢. You will see that together the two notes are worth \$2, but also worth four 50¢, and bear a ratio of 3:1.

A dotted quarter note	♩.	=	\$1.50	=	3 x 50¢
An eighth note	♪	=	50¢	=	2 x 25¢

The counting game

Every beat matters in music. Many impatient students hate waiting on longer notes and think it doesn't matter if they cut them short. Even a missing sixteenth note will throw the music out of synch.

Missed beats are like being shortchanged in a shop. So it is perhaps not unreasonable that students who persistently shortchange the music could be fined for each beat they miss, to be donated to the charity of their choice.

You can clarify tricky rhythms using these techniques:

• **Subdivide.** Choose a small unit for counting. If eighth notes predominate in this part of the music choose these as your currency. Then smaller black notes (sixteenths, thirty-seconds) seem less threatening when you slot them into frequent beats rather than try to fit a mass of notes into one long, bigger beat.

• **White-out.** Pieces which bristle with thick-tailed sixteenths, thirty-second notes or worse, like the snippet from Debussy's *Petite Piéce*, can be clarified by eliminating one set of tails – sixteenth notes are now eighths, quarter notes become half notes and so on.

You can do this with any difficult piece of music. Either write out a phrase, omitting one set of tails, or photocopy the section of your music and use white-out to erase one set of tails from notes. The threatening mass of tails becomes clearer and easier to decipher.

• **The "Automatic Ticker" in your head**. Imagine you have a metronome inside your head. Tick continuously through the subdivided beats in your head to make sense of their length and subdivisions.

• **Audible Ticker.** Play each subdivision by re-articulating a regular pulse through long notes. When this snippet of *When the Saints Go Marching In* is re-articulated (second line) the length of long notes becomes clear.

• **Catch words.** Less familiar patterns can be helped by making up words to go with them:

e.g.

triplets

Croc - o - dile or **pine - app - le**

dotted triplets

Ams - ter - dam or **kang - a - roo**

sixteenths

Cat - er - pill - ar or **Co - ca - Co - la**

• Say aloud or sing in the rhythm while you finger the notes.

• Rather than struggle to manage notes and rhythm at the same time, play just the rhythm on one repeated note or on empty ice-cream container bongo drums.

• Any syncopated rhythms seem more manageable if you practise by taking out the ties and re-articulating their notes as in this phrase from *In the Mood*:

• A sight reading quick-fix (especially useful with long bewildering passages of notes) is to take a few moments to pencil above the notes where the beats should fall, as in another excerpt from *In the Mood:*

There is no dogmatic "best" way. You might choose a combination of several systems: sometimes thinking "ta ta ti ti tiki tiki ta". Or you may prefer to count. Sometimes you might even choose to fiddle with the "correct" counting, for example thinking 1 2 3 4 5 on the long, tied notes in *When the Saints Go Marching In*, instead of 1 2 3 4 1 as it should be.

Who's to argue if it comes out correctly and clearly? Listeners can't hear what is happening inside your head.

The main thing is that you mentally tick through the beats, regularly and clearly. Choose whichever system works well for you.

Slow preparation will make rushing unlikely. When under pressure our heart pumps blood faster as a result of the adrenaline rush. Counter this natural inclination by thinking "slow and steady".

Another way to improve your rhythm is to play duets with a friend or tape one line of a duet and play along with it. If you don't play in time, any correct note in the wrong place is a mistake, just as a weed is a plant growing where it shouldn't. All those correct notes you learned so carefully need to be placed in the right part of the bar.

Sight reading with friends or playing in an ensemble gives you scope to develop the useful skill of keeping going when lost, listening and jumping to the correct bar.

If you don't develop a satisfactory system to keep time your playing will be stilted and listeners (including teachers and examiners) will notice.

When you solve any rhythmic glitches your music will flow.

- Gazing at the music while practising meditation
- Play too fast, get into a muddle and have to undo bad mistakes
- Time how long it takes for a full circuit of the piano stool
- Scooby-dooby doodling around

Chapter 5

The dirtiest word of all: Scales

The music prodigy Anton Rubenstein used to practise his scales with his nose in a novel. However, later in life, he admitted he wished he had worked more seriously earlier (and with less raging – but that's another story).

Who wants to spend time on boring aspects like scales? Many students waste time trundling through a maze of notes while thinking of something more interesting. They may make the same mistakes every time, reinforcing them until they become part of the plot.

Well, you do warm up before your triathalon or game of

basketball or soccer, don't you? Think of scales as warm-ups, to get your fingers loosened and working well.

So, why practise scales?

Look at this excerpt from Mozart's Clarinet Concerto.

It is a mix of scales here, arpeggios there, a dominant 7th chord, a touch of chromatic and a trill to add attitude. If you have practised relevant scales and arpeggios before turning to the concerto you can let your musicianship flow and enjoy the piece.

Once, while a university student, I was rather miffed when a listener overheard my erratic practice of scales and commented that I "made so many mistakes!" Looking back, she was right. I was playing mindlessly, probably learning more mistakes than correct notes. Why waste time and energy treading the mistakes deeper into the bog? The problem is that I really did not know then how to get the wretched things better.

My major reason was that scales make little sense on a clarinet, unlike the piano, where you can see the notes and the scale patterns there in front of you. A keyboard player routinely produces new intervals of varied width by moving just one finger. The clarinettist may move three, or even all 10, but with illogical results; move one thumb and leap an interval of 12 notes, yet a half-tone's difference can be produced by moving three fingers.

At least woodwind players lift or drop their fingers according to whether the pitch ascends or descends. Mostly. Pity the trumpeters – there is no such logic in their finger movements. String players follow patterns, while relying largely on their ear. Players of all other instruments except piano are largely without visible structures to guide them. They continually have to think what comes next, note by note, and rely on knowledge of key signatures.

Give the notes their correct names

Sure, you flinch at the uncommon accidentals like G♭, C♭, A♯, B♯ and E♯. Not to mention double sharps or double flats! Many young players try to simplify enharmonic changes by converting them to the familiar version.

Notes, like people, have two names. You wouldn't like to be called by your middle name, would you? It is essential to give notes their correct names according to the key, mode or tonal centre, even if it means facing seemingly unnatural names. This also keeps the integrity of the harmony. The dual names of notes are illustrated below:

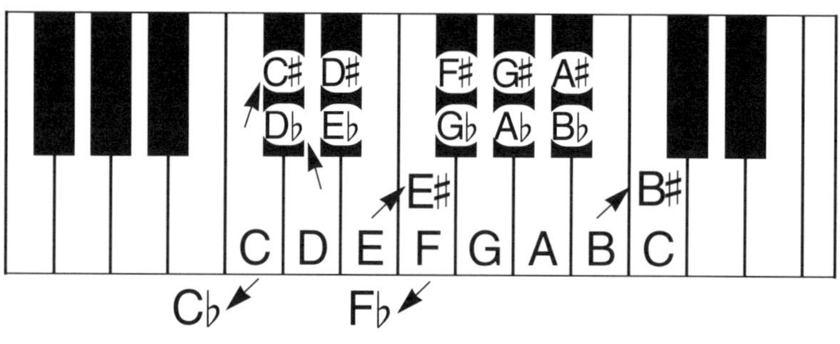

Enharmonic names of notes

Many students avoid the naming issue altogether; they manage instead to play the scales quite reasonably by ear at home, when relaxed. In the exam room they grope through the fog which encircles their mind, eyes and ears. At times like this, turning E♯ into F falls down. Under pressure, the brain argues with itself: "Hey, how can there be F as well as F♯ in the same scale?" By which time you have faltered, stumbled, lost the track – and your confidence.

And, do you remember that confusion, the way you chastised

yourself every time you botched it up? Your brain does. So, every time you play F♯ minor incorrectly, you spread another misty layer of negative memory over it. This is what the brain remembers when under pressure in an exam. If you started learning the scale in a rushed, unthinking way, riddled with mistakes, you need to re-program your brain. Play it correctly and slowly enough times to clarify it. Remember: repeat an action 50 times to fix a habit.

Ensure fluent scales in exams

Start regular daily practice of the technical requirements today. The month or the week before an exam will be too late and resulting tension and panic will turn your fingers rigid like barb-wire. It is far easier to comfortably and thoroughly learn one scale a week, with all their accompanying minors, arpeggios and other chords. If you cram them all into your head at the last minute you will play them riddled with mistakes. They will sound like a frenetic pinball game – kerplunk … zonk … pow.

Each time you play a scale correctly you are reinforcing it with positive memories of success. If your brain has been correctly programmed you do not need to fear a few moments' panic in an exam. You go into auto-drive and your fingers move automatically until the fog in your mind clears.

Therein lies confidence!

Excuses, excuses…

- I did so much writing at school, my fingers are sore
- I lost the key to the piano
- Our dog howls when I play
- But I know that scale now
- My trumpet got abducted by aliens
- I fell off the bus, and it ran over my clarinet
- I couldn't hear the TV so I had to stop
- My brother paid me to not practise

The Circle of Fifths

We can demystify scales by understanding that they are built on a logical pattern which is illustrated by the "circle of fifths".

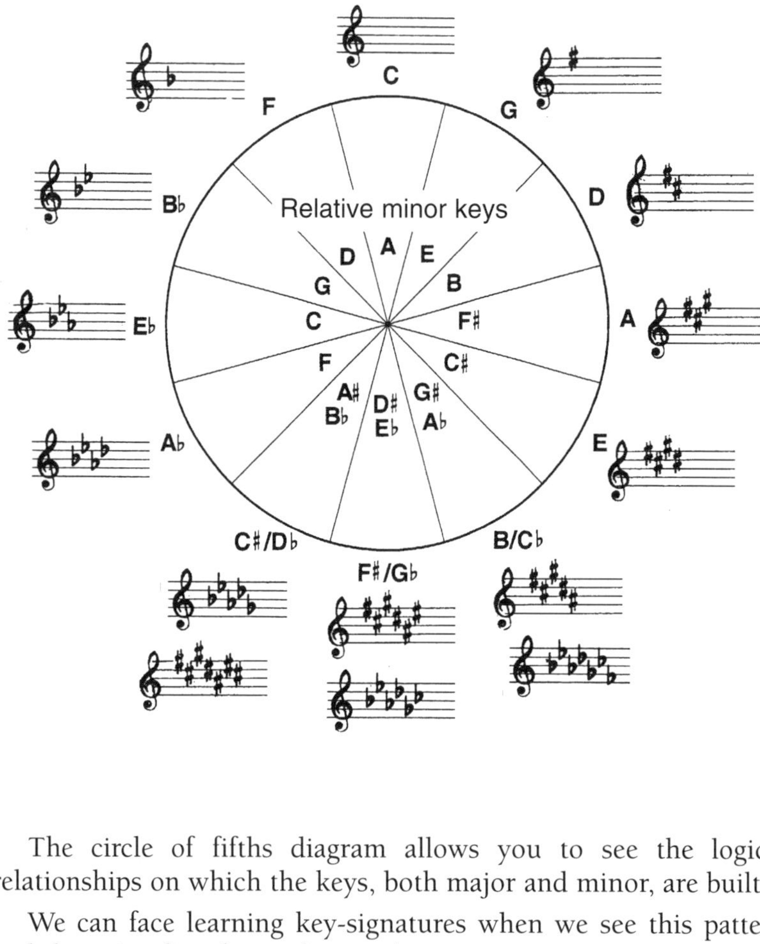

The circle of fifths diagram allows you to see the logical relationships on which the keys, both major and minor, are built.

We can face learning key-signatures when we see this pattern and then visualise them when under pressure.

Start with C major (at the top) which has no sharps or flats. Move clockwise five notes (a fifth) at a time to add each new sharp key in turn. For flat keys, move anti-clockwise from C major down a fifth at a time. Inside the circle is each major key's related minor scale.

Each new key adds a sharp or a flat according to a strict order of sharps and flats. The order of sharps is: F♯, C♯, G♯, D♯, A♯, E♯ and B♯. Remember this pattern by thinking either "Fast Cars Go Driving Around East Bolivia" or "Fraught Conductors Get Diarrhoea After Eating Breakfast". The order of flats is the reverse of the sharps: B♭, E♭, A♭, D♭, G♭, C♭, and F♭ ("Big Eaters Always Devour Green Cooked Fettuccine").

Foolproof ways to practise major and minor scales

Scales are relatively simple as long as the signposts of key signatures are followed. Here is the scale of G major in a simple, non-manuscript, graphic form. These scale graphics can be used for scales on any instrument, including the voice.

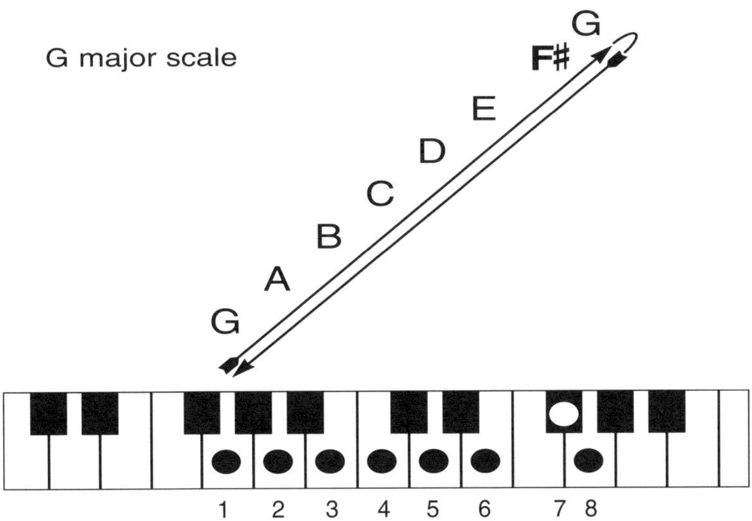

G major's arpeggio simply takes the first, third and fifth notes, repeats the key note (the tonic) then returns as the diagram below shows.

G major arpeggio

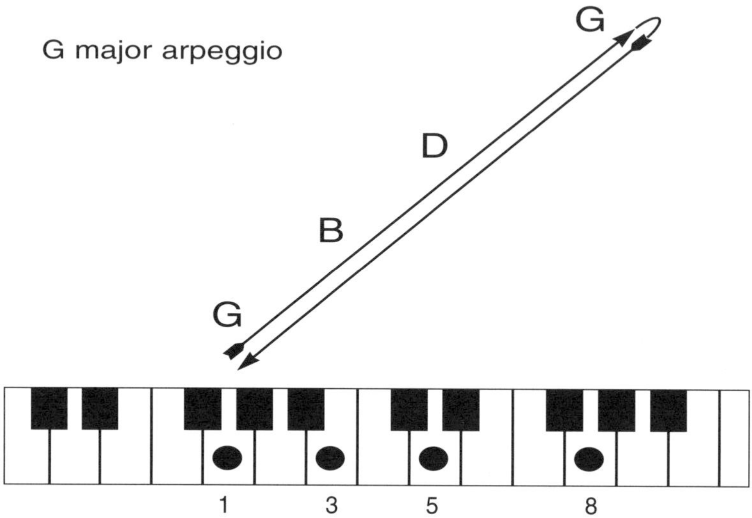

The difference between major and minor scales lies in the structure of tones and semitones which create distinctively different moods – happy for major and sad for minor.

To complicate things even more, we play two forms of minor scales – harmonic and melodic, which developed from the earlier natural minor scale A B C D E F G A. It is not surprising that some learners often put the difficult minor scales in the too-hard basket. But in an exam room, they do not conveniently disappear.

Here's how harmonic minor scales work: The most important note in a minor scale, that makes it sound gloomy, is the 7th note. It's called the "Leading Note" because it leads to the keynote (tonic). It always rises a half-tone above that of the natural minor.

Play this on your instrument: **A B C D E F G#**

You can hear that it sounds unfinished, that it needs a last note.

The story goes that Wolfgang Amadeus Mozart didn't like getting up at 5am on cold snowy Salzburg mornings to practise. His father Leopold, a canny teacher, solved the problem by playing as loudly as possible on the harpsichord:

A B C D E F G# ...

Poor little Wolfgang could not stand it. He would throw on his slippers and dressing gown, run down the stairs and play the tonic:

A

What drove young Wolfgang was that a harmonic minor scale which hangs unresolved on the sharpened 7th note is pure agony to the ear and demands completion with the keynote.

These 7th and 8th notes are the most important in a harmonic minor scale.

In all harmonic minor scales the 7th note is always raised. (Illustrated with a bump in the line – like a speed bump on a road.) This is seen in the following A harmonic minor scale.

Excuses, excuses…

- Dad said I should know it all by now
- By the time I get to do my practice it's too late and the neighbours call the police
- None of my friends have to
- I'm the only one in the whole street who's forced to practise
- My sister has just started learning the same instrument and I don't want her to be disheartened by hearing me sound better
- Every time I start to play, the baby throws up
- When I practise it only gets worse
- My Mum had a migraine all week
- I left my instrument on the bus
- My baby sister ate my only saxophone reed
- My cat bites me when I play high notes

A harmonic minor

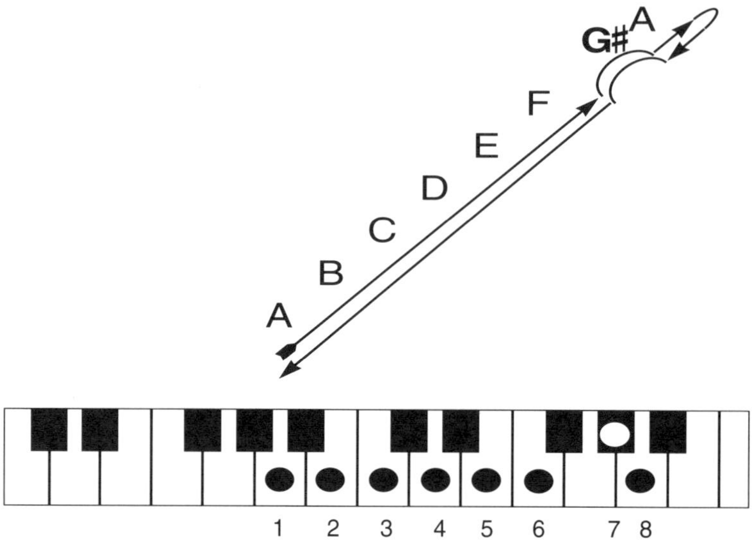

The melodic has two speed bumps ascending, on the sixth and 7th notes. They return by the smoother route of the natural minor, without the speed bumps.

A melodic minor

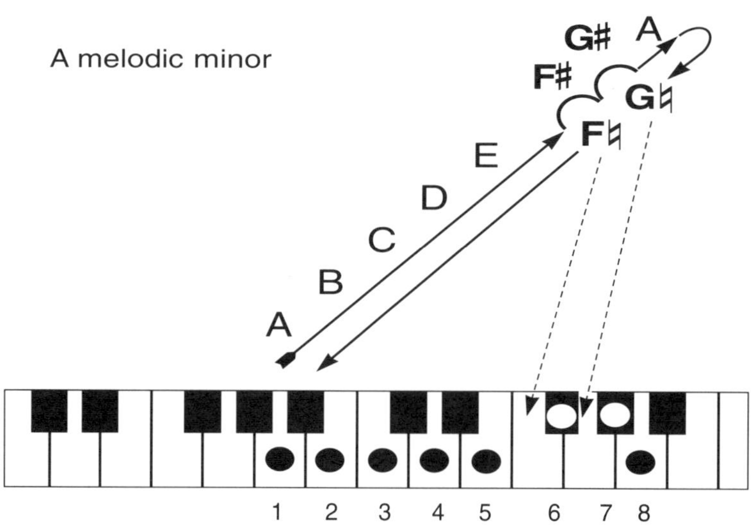

What is crucial to minor scales is that the raised 7th resolves to the tonic by a semitone. Whatever else you miss, make sure you get the leading note right – raised by a half-tone.

The 6th, 7th and 8th notes, the tip of the iceberg, need most of your attention. Then add-a-note, progressively down the scale. If you do 80% of your practice here at the tip, the rest comes easily.

Take one octave at a time. Say aloud and finger. Then play SLOWLY. Set yourself up for success. You managed it correctly? Congratulate yourself. Play it again to prove it's no big deal.

Practise the next octave of the scale similarly. When secure, join the two together. Work on a third octave separately. Join.

Scale structures

It is valuable to know the format of the scales. All major scales are constructed using the pattern of tones and half-tones (semitones):

tone – tone – half-tone – tone – tone – tone – half-tone

All harmonic minor scales use the structure:

tone – half-tone – tone – tone – half-tone – tone-and-a-half – half-tone

Excuses, excuses...

- My strings are rusty, I worried I might cut myself
- I don't know how to tune my violin
- I spilt acid on my hands in chemistry then rubbed my eyes
- My finger hurts, maybe I have arthritis.
- My scales grew fins, then gills as well, then turned into a fish and swam away in the river of saliva that collects at the bottom of the tuning slide

The spacings of tones and half-tones are clear in these illustrations of E minor harmonic and melodic.

E harmonic minor

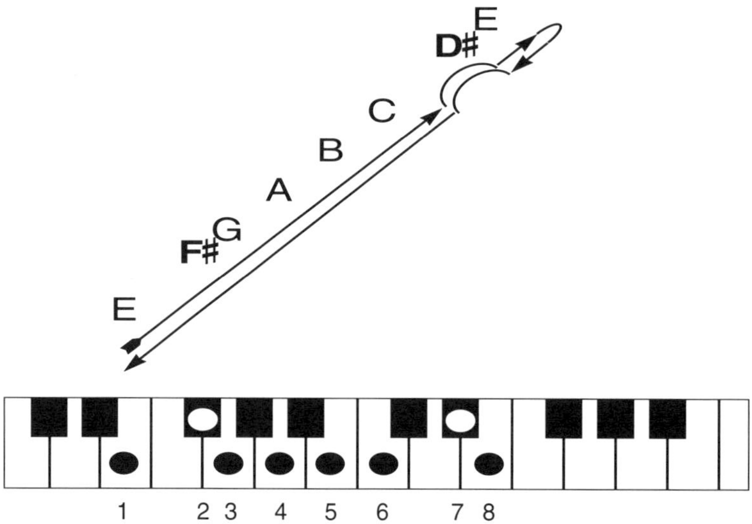

E melodic minor

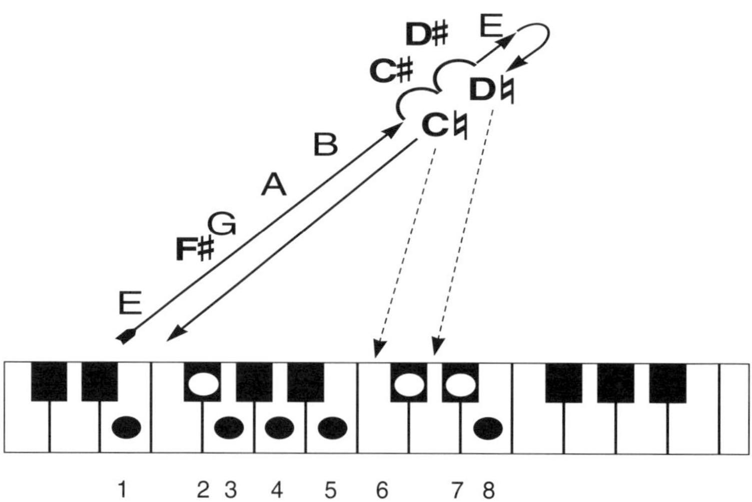

The melodic minor's structure, on the other hand, consists of:

tone – half-tone – tone – tone – tone – tone – half-tone

But the raised 6th and 7th notes are lowered on the descent.

This system of structures is utilised effectively by string players who think in patterns rather than keys.

Facing difficult scales

Scales with a couple of sharps or flats can usually be faced by most students. Using our visual method, reinforced by a knowledge of the scales' underlying structure, we can tackle the more mean or exotic keys which bristle with sharps and flats.

This graphic method can be applied to all aspects of learning scales and other technical work. The alternative, rote playing from scale books, often merely dulls the brain. When we read scales from a book, our brain may snooze onto auto-pilot. It is possible to play this way quite successfully – until we shut the book.

Replicating the pattern for all major scales means that seemingly fierce keys, bristling with sharps, actually make sense when seen on the keyboard. For example, the scale of B major.

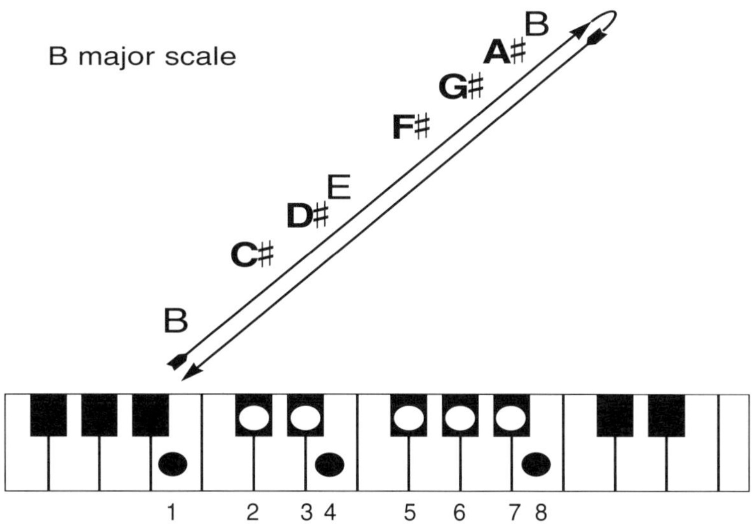

Let's pick a mean looking scale – G♯ melodic minor, which is related to B major. We will learn it correctly, comfortably and thoroughly, so when the examiner asks for it, you could almost laugh out aloud.

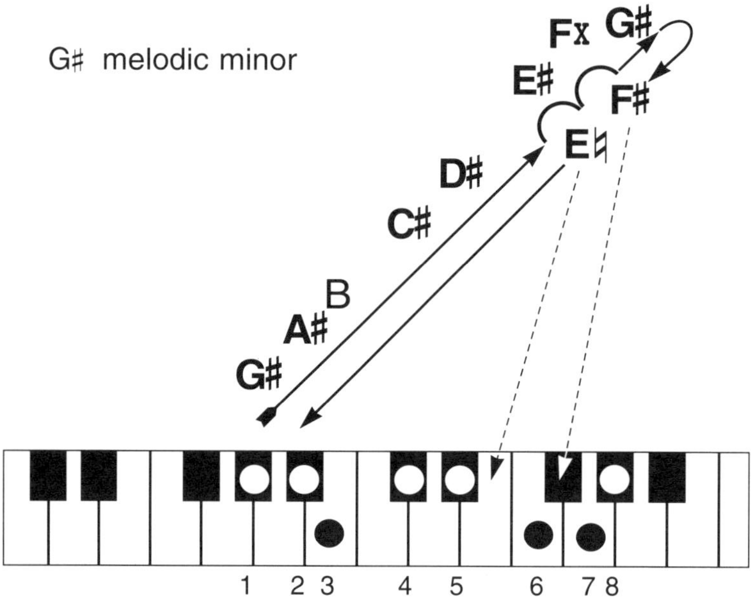

- Check the key signature: F♯, C♯, G♯, D♯, A♯.
- Highlight or red pencil any accidentals and odd notes such as Fx (F♯ sharpened again).
- Say the notes of one octave aloud while fingering, looking each note square in the eye. Repeat.
- Play the scale at a crawl. Leave one note only when you know where you are heading.
- Pat yourself on the back! Say aloud, "I did it! I played G♯ melodic correctly!"
- But did you play in a soft, tentative tone? Now, play it *fortissimo*, big and bold and confidently.
- Much better. Repeat. Relish your success.

• When you're confident, try memorising it. Shut your eyes and, without playing, say the notes aloud while fingering. Note any hesitations.

• Play it slowly from memory. Congratulate yourself. Do the same for the next octave.

Each time you succeed you are reinforcing that scale with positive memories.

Draw up a large wall-chart, with columns for all sections of the technical requirements, a box for every single item. While practising, write in fingerings or unusual patterns.

Reward yourself for mastering each section.

Key signatures and accidentals

You can apply the tip-of-the-iceberg concept in playing minor scales by referring to the following eight pages.

These pages list each scale's key signature and all accidentals which make up its related minor scales, both harmonic and melodic.

The first line on the first two pages looks like this:

KEY SIGNATURE	MAJOR SCALE	HARMONIC MINOR SCALE	RAISED 7th	MELODIC MINOR SCALE	RAISED 6th & 7th	PATTERN OF ACCIDENTALS
	C	A	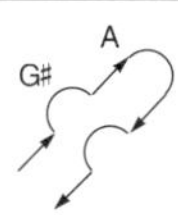	A	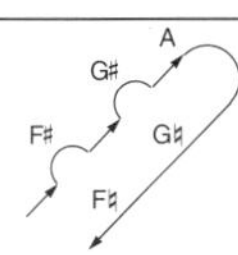	

It covers C major and its relative A minor, with their key signature (no sharps or flats in this case). The fourth column shows A harmonic minor's leading note (G♯) and the sixth column shows the melodic minor form with its 6th and 7th raised on the ascent then lowered on the descent. The last column shows a simplified pattern of the accidentals for the melodic.

With these charts of key signatures and accidentals for all keys, both flats and sharps, you can face and work out even the most advanced and difficult scales.

Major, harmonic and melodic minor

KEY SIGNATURE	MAJOR SCALE	HARMONIC MINOR SCALE	RAISED 7th	
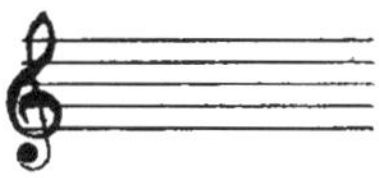	C	A	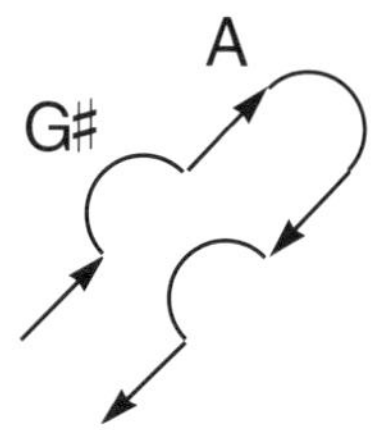	
	G	E	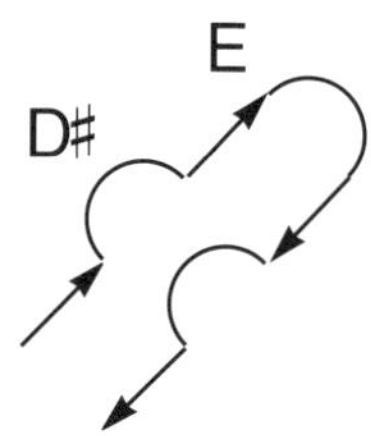	
	D	B	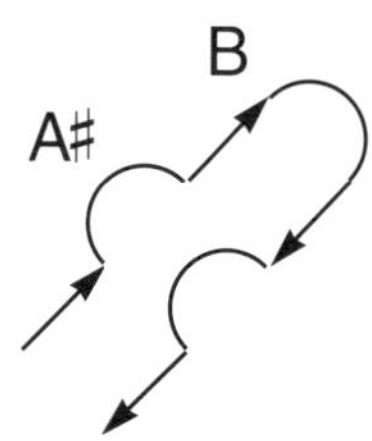	
	A	F♯	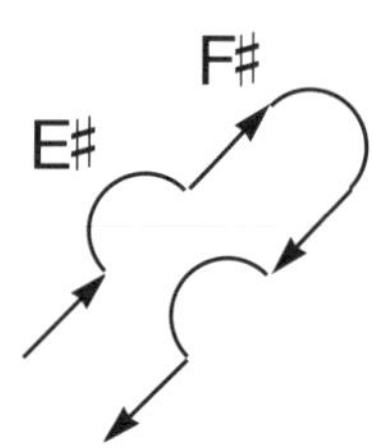	

scales – up to three sharp keys

	MELODIC MINOR SCALE	RAISED 6th & 7th	PATTERN OF ACCIDENTALS
	A	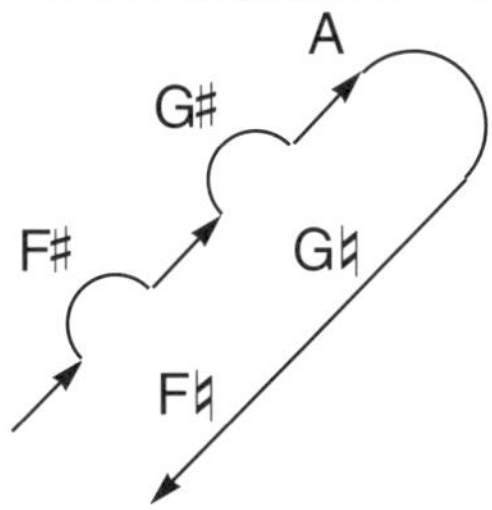	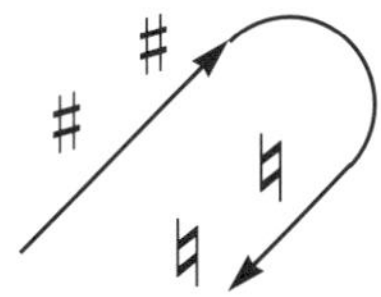
	E	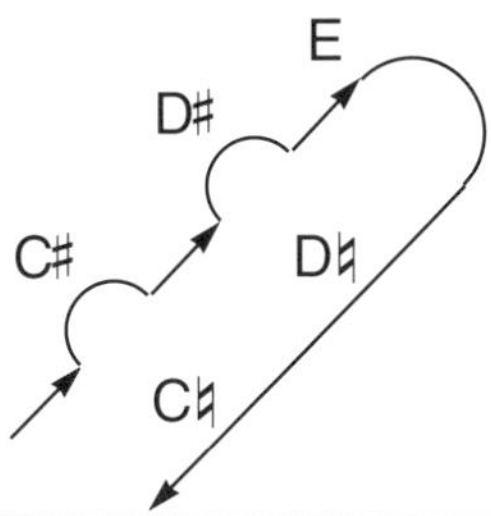	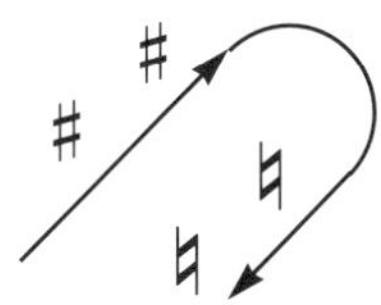
	B	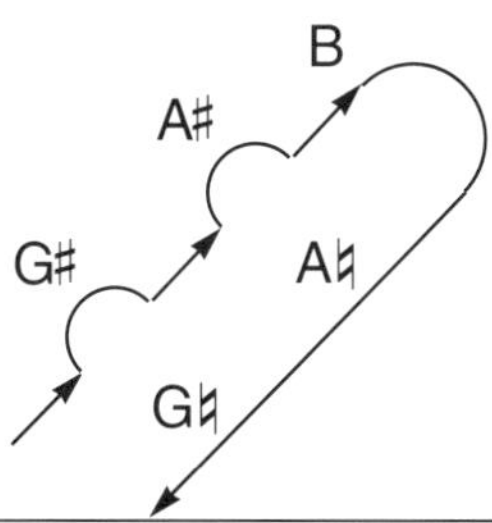	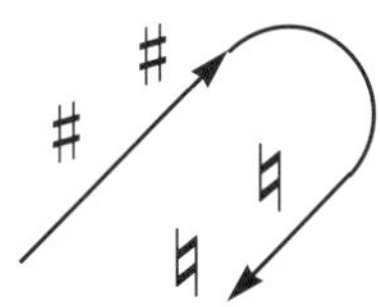
	F♯	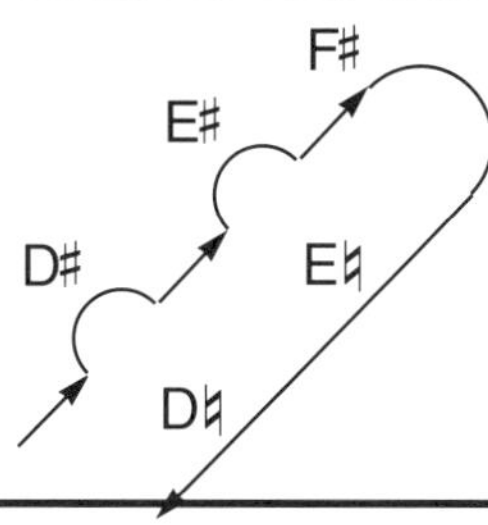	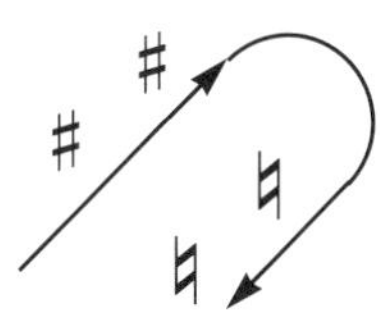

Major, harmonic and melodic minor

KEY SIGNATURE	MAJOR SCALE	HARMONIC MINOR SCALE	RAISED 7th	
	E	C♯	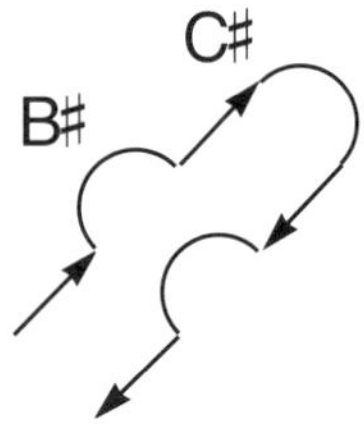	
	B	G♯	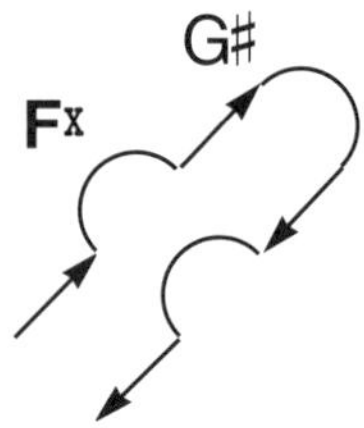	
	F♯	D♯	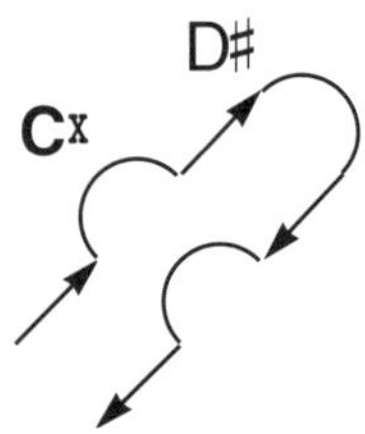	
	C♯	A♯	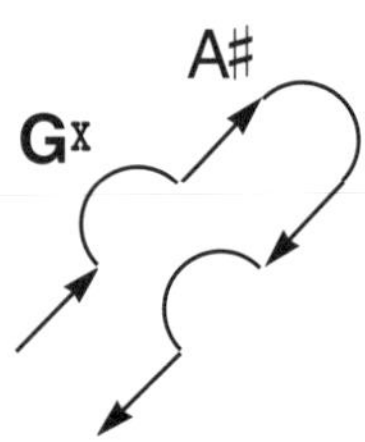	

scales – four to seven sharp keys

	MELODIC MINOR SCALE	RAISED 6th & 7th	PATTERN OF ACCIDENTALS
	C♯	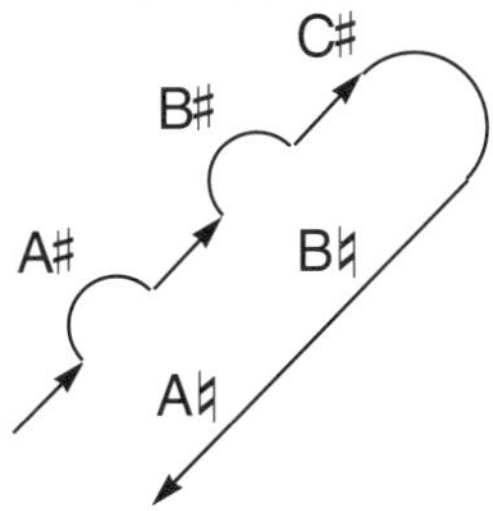	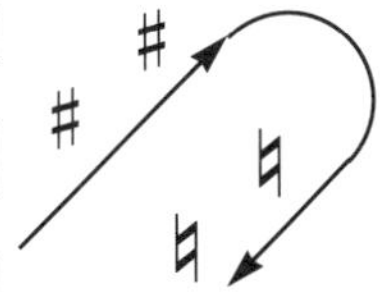
	G♯	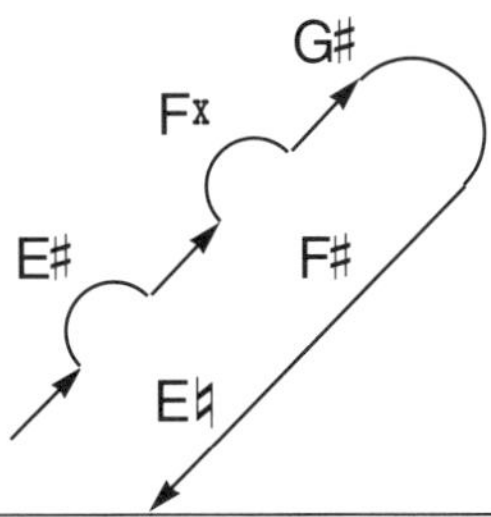	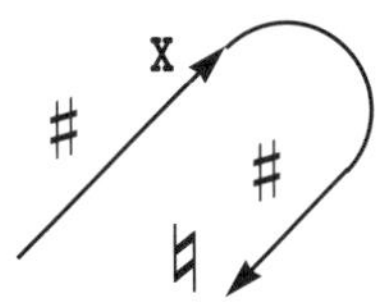
	D♯	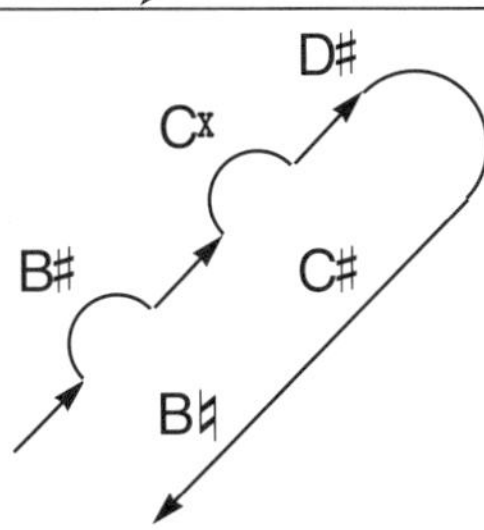	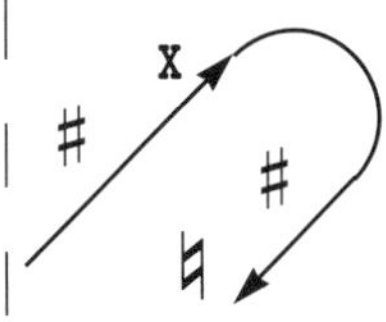
	A♯	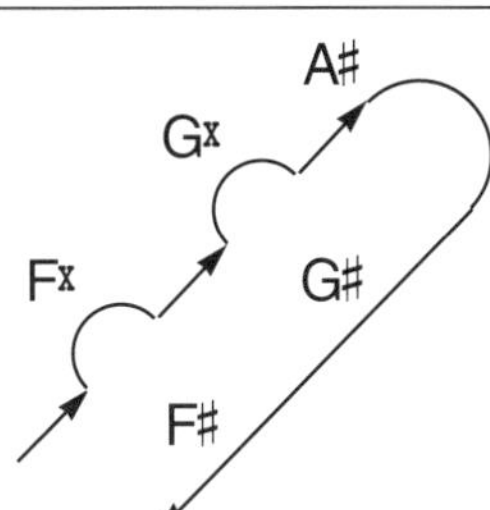	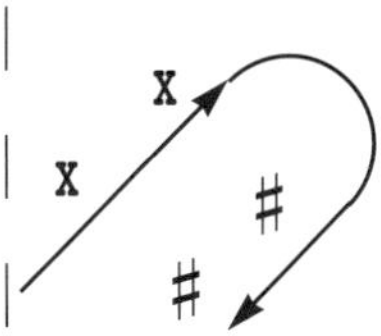

Major, harmonic and melodic minor

KEY SIGNATURE	MAJOR SCALE	HARMONIC MINOR SCALE	RAISED 7th	
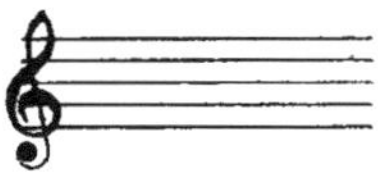	C	A	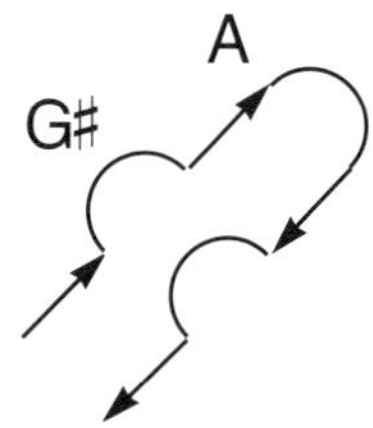	
	F	D	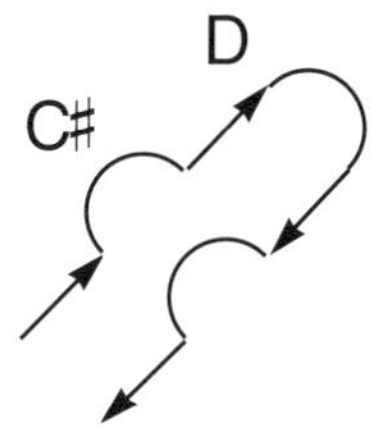	
	B♭	G	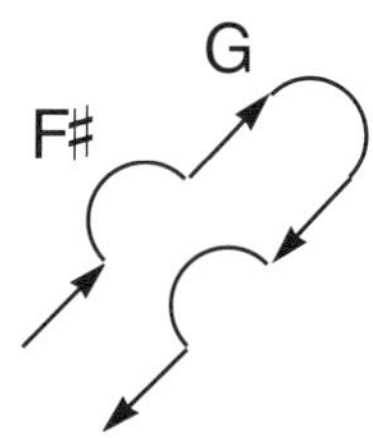	
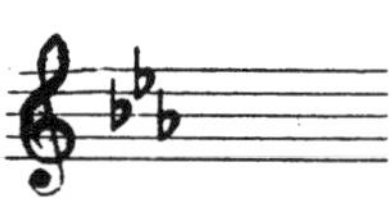	E♭	C	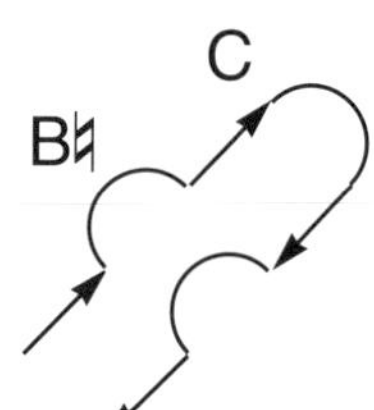	

scales – up to three flat keys

MELODIC MINOR SCALE	RAISED 6th & 7th	PATTERN OF ACCIDENTALS
A	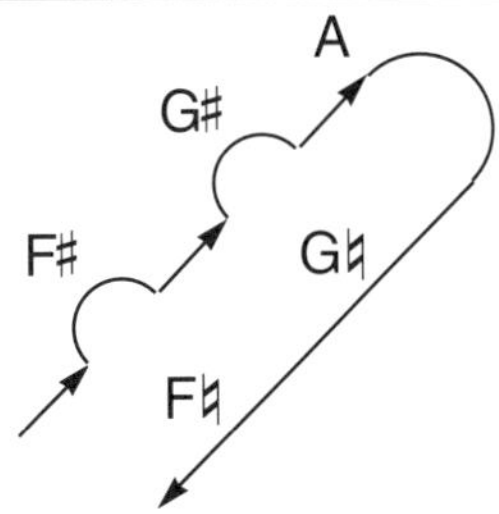	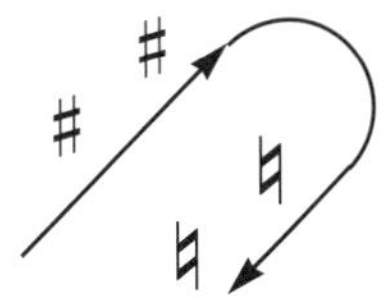
D	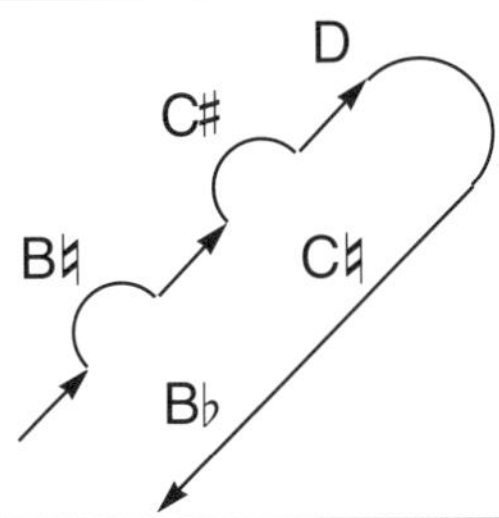	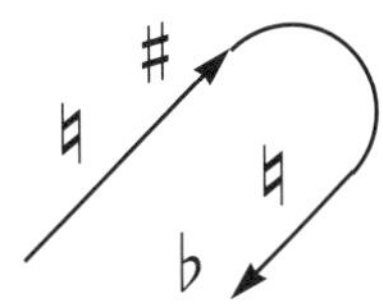
G	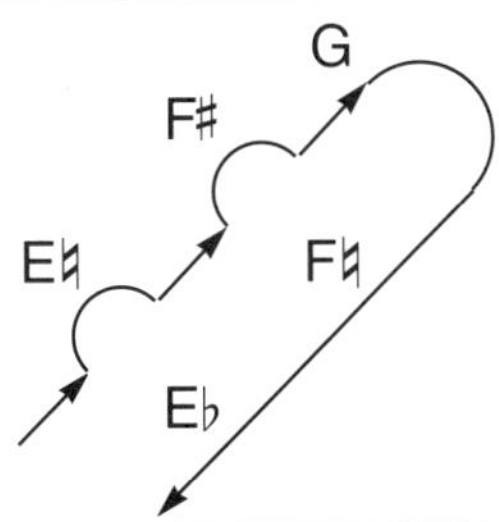	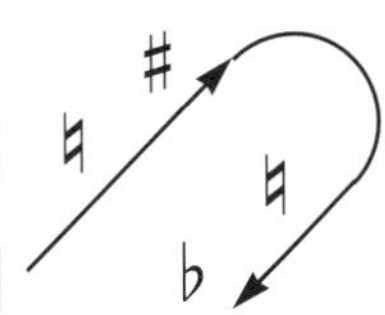
C	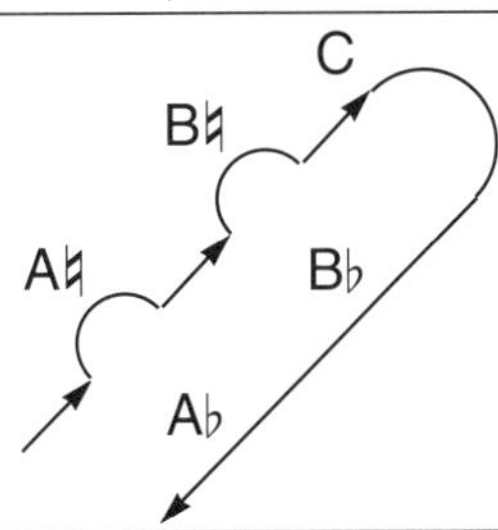	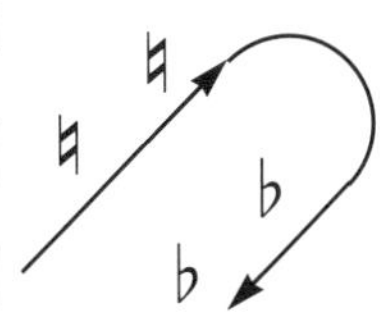

Major, harmonic and melodic minor

KEY SIGNATURE	MAJOR SCALE	HARMONIC MINOR SCALE	RAISED 7th	
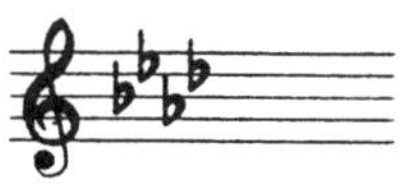	A♭	F	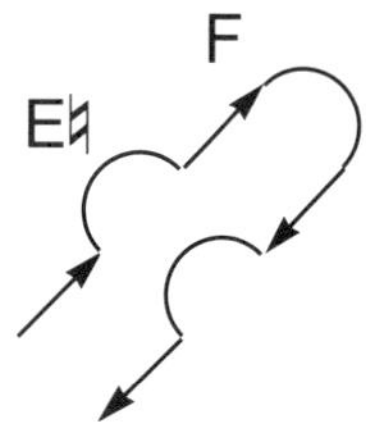	
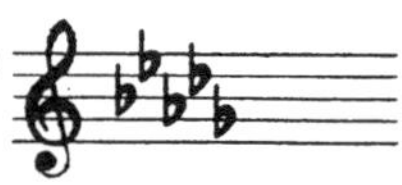	D♭	B♭	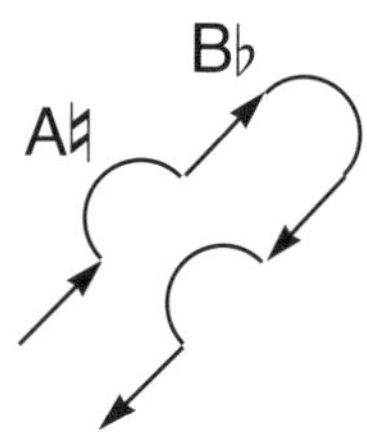	
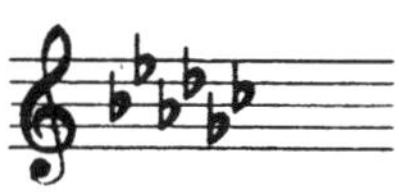	G♭	E♭	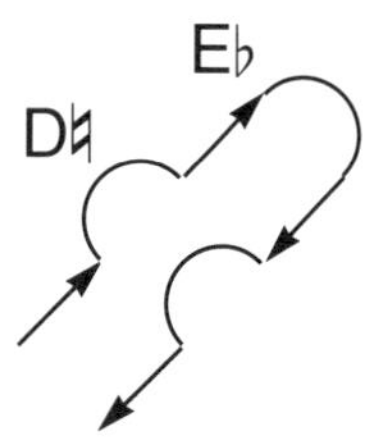	
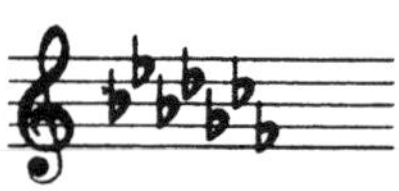	C♭	A♭	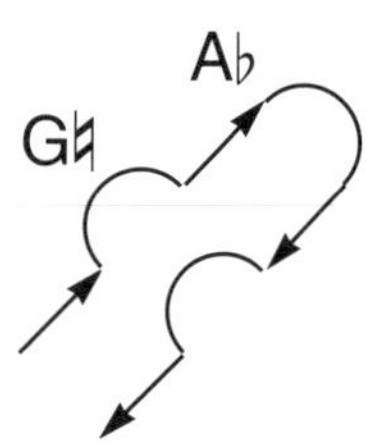	

scales – four to seven flat keys

	MELODIC MINOR SCALE	RAISED 6th & 7th	PATTERN OF ACCIDENTALS
	F	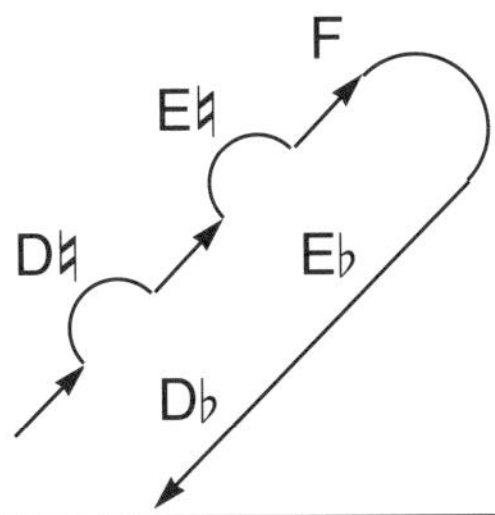	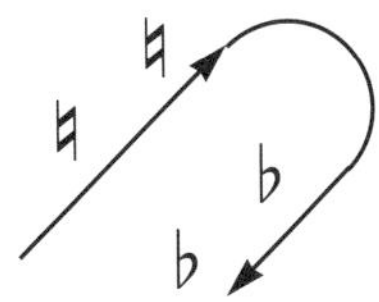
	B♭	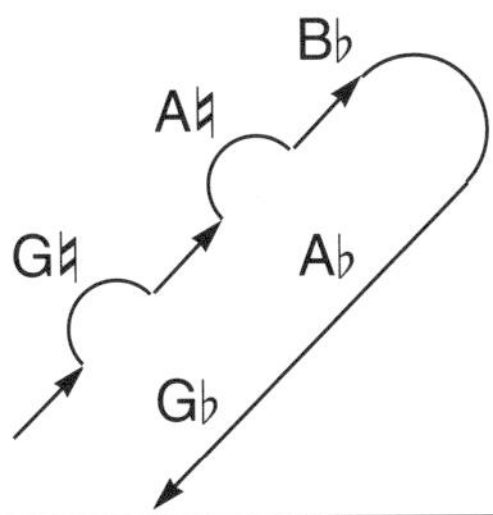	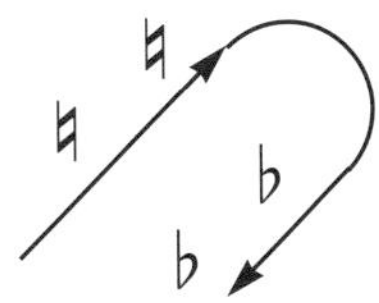
	E♭	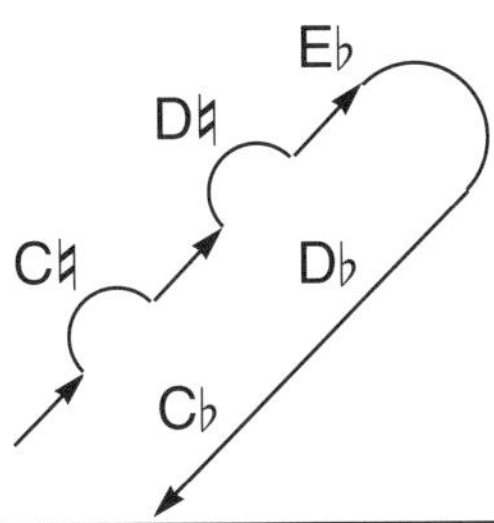	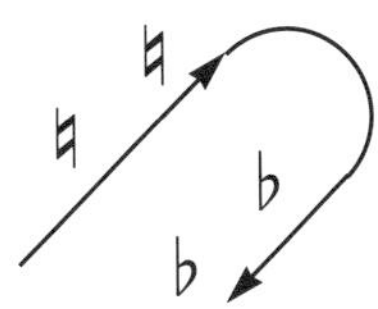
	A♭	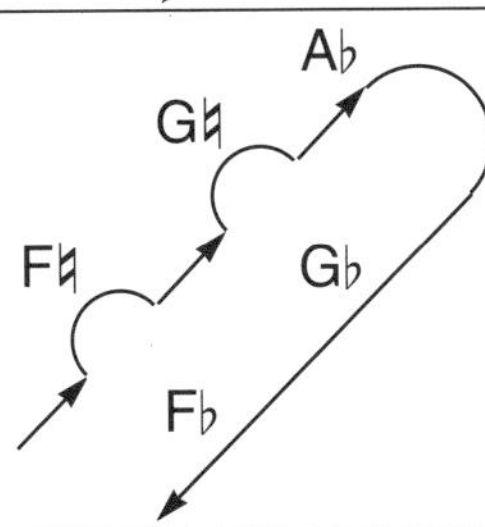	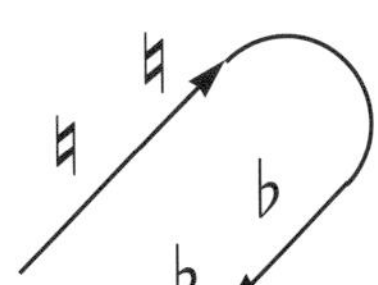

Let us extend the visual method to find some foolproof ways of learning arpeggios, dominant 7th chords, diminished 7th chords, whole-tone scales and chromatic scales.

Arpeggios

Every scale has a related arpeggio. Arpeggios are simply chords played note after note. They consist of the first, third and fifth notes of the scale with the tonic note repeated at the top after a wider interval.

Arpeggios are more straight forward for keyboard players because they can see the pattern. Many players of other instruments memorise the letter names of the ascending notes but forget to reverse them for the descent. These are quite simple if you see the notes set out clearly like this B major arpeggio:

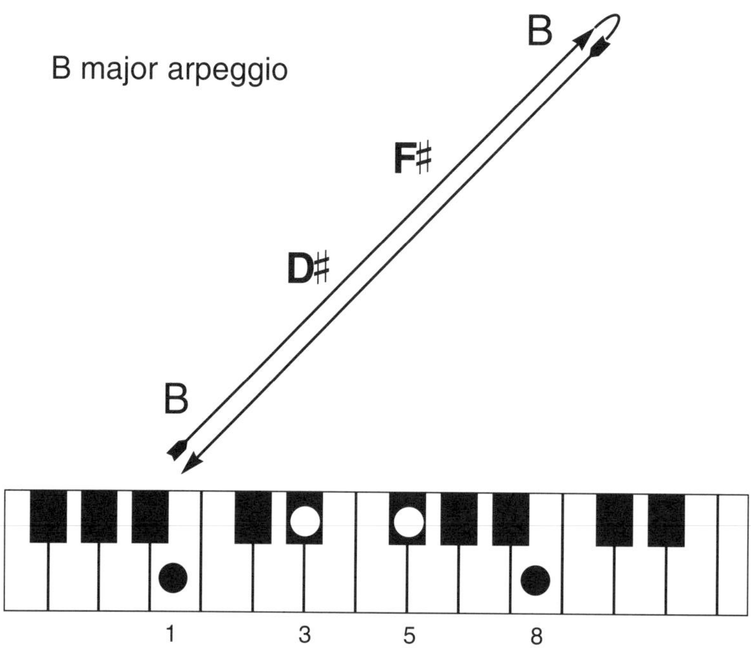

Learn one octave at a time, then join them.

The difference between a major and a minor arpeggio is always that the second note played is a half-tone lower for the minor. For example, G major arpeggio (page 50) consists of G B D G compared with G minor's G B♭ D G.

B major's relative minor arpeggio is G# minor:

G# minor arpeggio

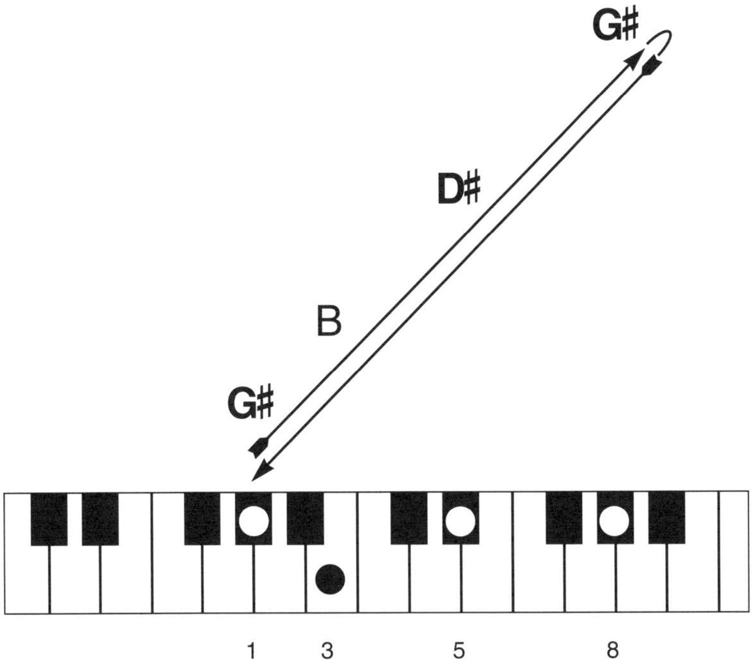

Dominant 7th chords

A dominant 7th chord is a major triad (arpeggio) with an added minor 7th note. The "dominant" refers to the fact that we build this chord on the fifth note of the scale in that particular key.

Dominant 7ths may seem baffling because they start on a note other than the keynote (tonic). This often flummoxes students if they mistake the starting note for the keynote, losing sight of the key signature.

The format of dominant 7ths is best explained at the keyboard to show the relationship of the tonic and dominant:

Let's pick an easy key – C major, illustrated on the keyboard below. The tonic chord of C major is C E G. We start on the fifth (dominant) note G and build a chord G B D. Then we add the 7th note, F, continue up to G, and come back. We resolve to the tonic, C, an interval of a Perfect 4th higher.

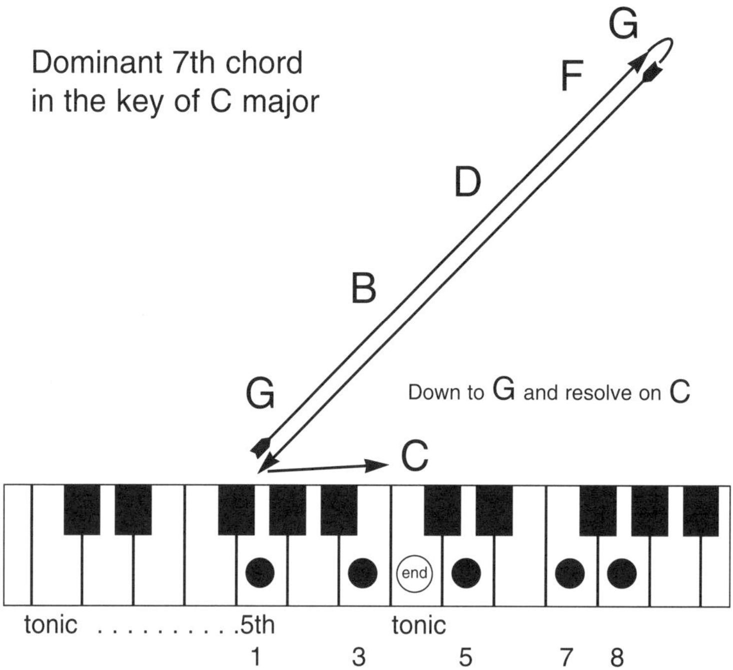

We can think of the Dominant 7th as G major arpeggio with a flattened 7th. However, with Dominant 7ths, it is crucial to remember which key you are playing in. Thus the Dominant 7th in the key of C major (above) has F♮, rather than the F♯ that would be found in G major (below). The Dominant 7th of G major has C♮, rather than the C♯ found in D major.

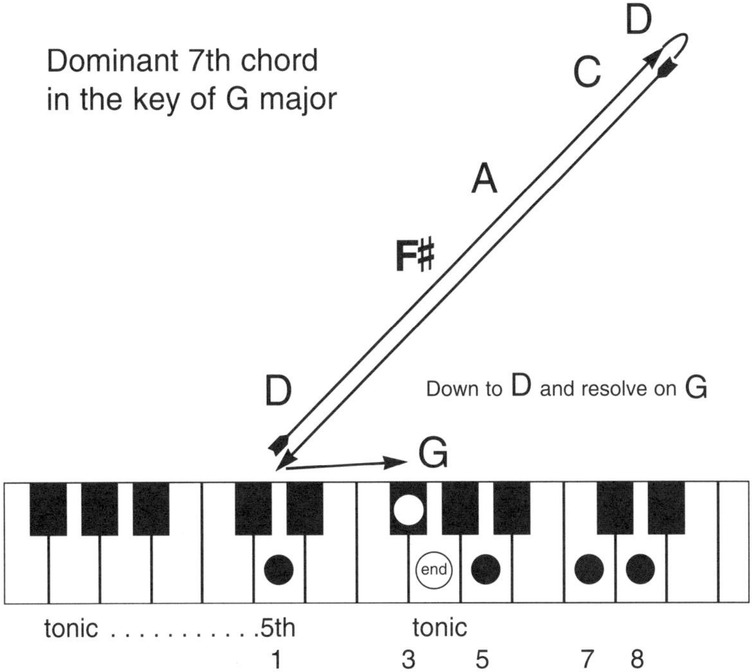

G major chord is G B D. We start on the fifth note D, the dominant, and build a chord D F♯ A. Then we add the 7th note, C, continue up to D, and come back. We resolve to the tonic, G.

Diminished 7th chords

Diminished 7th chords consist of superimposed minor 3rd intervals. They are close cousins of each key's Dominant 7th chord. Of their total five notes, they have three in common, as well as resolving to the same tonic. Diminished 7th chords start on the second note of their related Dominant 7th, they copy the next two notes, a minor third is added, the starting is doubled. They return, and resolve to their tonic.

For example, when the Diminished 7th chord of G is compared to the Dominant 7th of G major the relationship becomes clear:

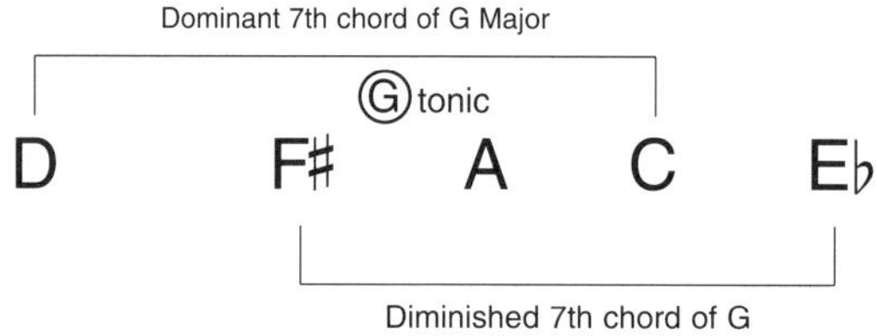

The Diminished 7th starts on the second note of the Dominant 7th chord (F♯). Then play A C and add another note a minor third higher, E♭.

The illustration below shows the Diminished 7th chord of G in full. After the first four notes, double the starting note (F♯) at the top, return (E♭ C A) to the starting note F♯, then resolve up a semitone to the tonic G.

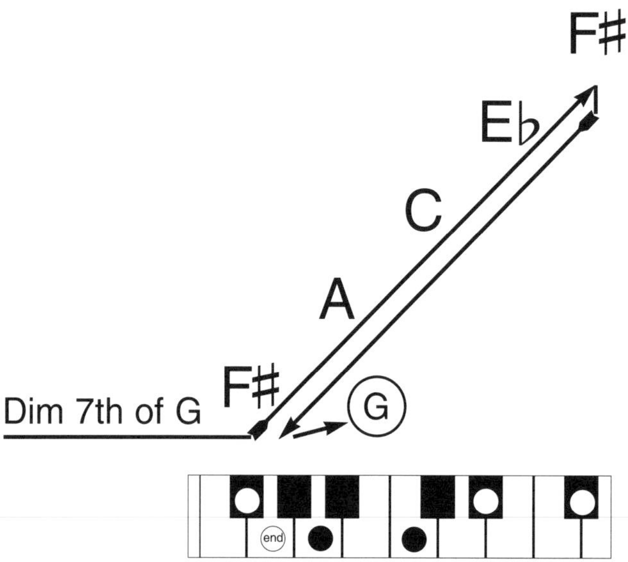

This pattern is described as being "of G" rather than "in the key of G major" as Dominant 7ths are described. Diminished 7th chords derive from minor keys or from tonal centres and are constructed of a series of minor third intervals.

In manuscript form in a traditional scale book (as shown below), the chords or arpeggios of the Diminished 7th are a bewildering mass of sharps, flats and other accidentals. While it is possible to play them by automatically following the notes, the student might not understand their simple structures and relationships and might have difficulty playing them from memory in an examination.

To construct a Diminished 7th chord:

- Begin on the seventh note of the minor key (always a half-tone lower than the tonic).
- Build a triad consisting of a series of minor thirds.
- Double the starting note.
- Return to the starting note in reverse order.
- Resolve up a half-tone to the tonic.

The 12 Diminished 7th chords can be divided into three groups of four, shown on the following three pages as Patterns No.1, No.2 and No.3. Each group has the same four notes, irrespective of their enharmonic names. The starting note rotates according to the key. The keyboards show the even spacings of consistent minor third intervals (i.e. three half-tones) that typify all Diminished 7ths.

Chords of Diminished 7ths, Pattern No.1

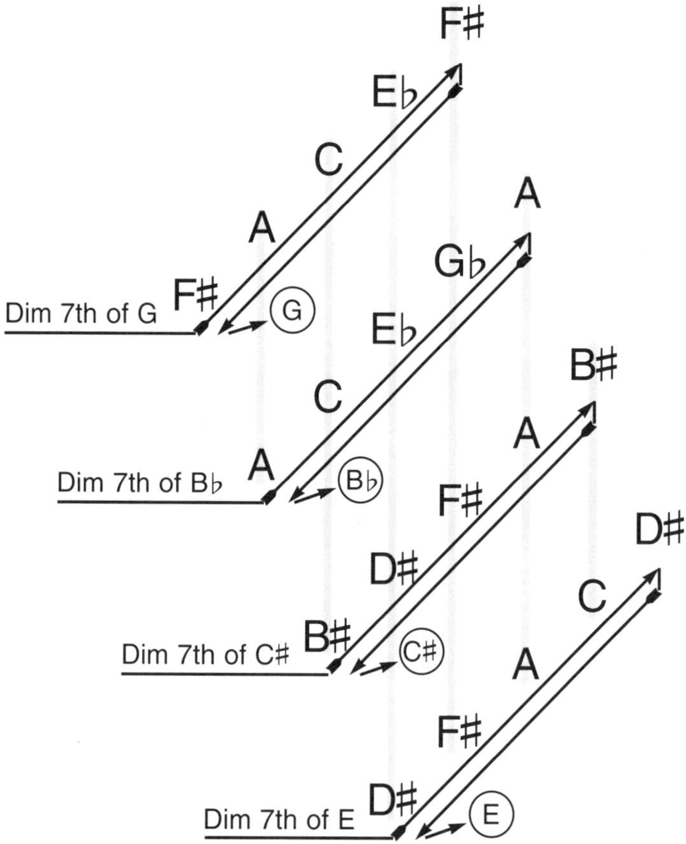

The keyboard below shows that the four chords of Pattern No.1 are created using just four notes, whatever their enharmonic name. (For each chord, the starting note is doubled at the top.)

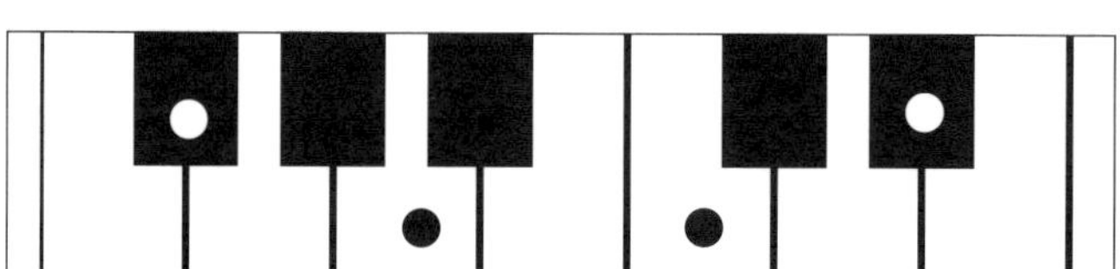

Chords of Diminished 7ths, Pattern No.2

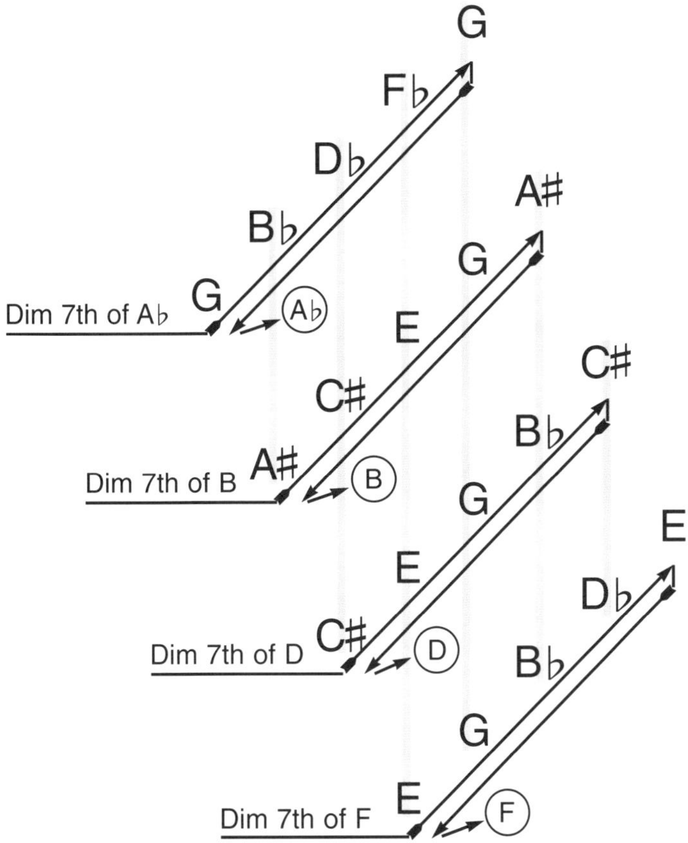

The keyboard below shows that the four chords of Pattern No.2 are created using just four notes, whatever their enharmonic name. (For each chord, the starting note is doubled at the top.)

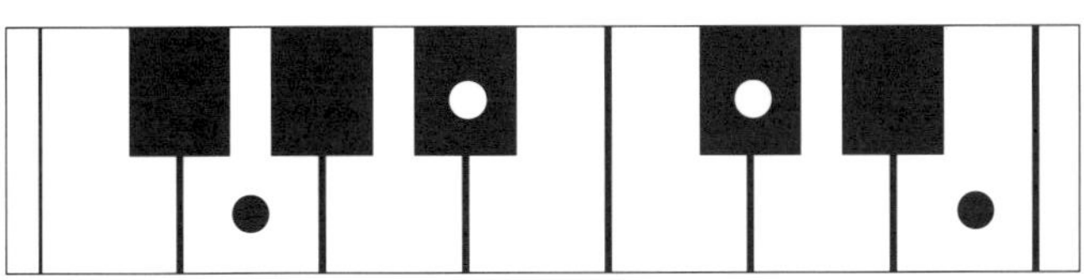

Chords of Diminished 7ths, Pattern No.3

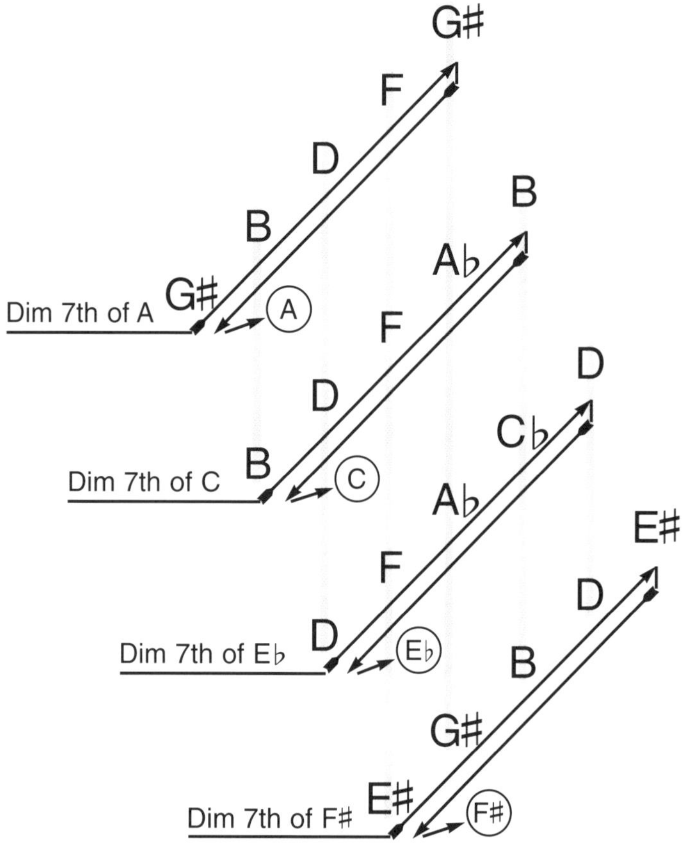

The keyboard below shows that the four chords of Pattern No.3 are created using just four notes, whatever their enharmonic name. (For each chord, the starting note is doubled at the top.)

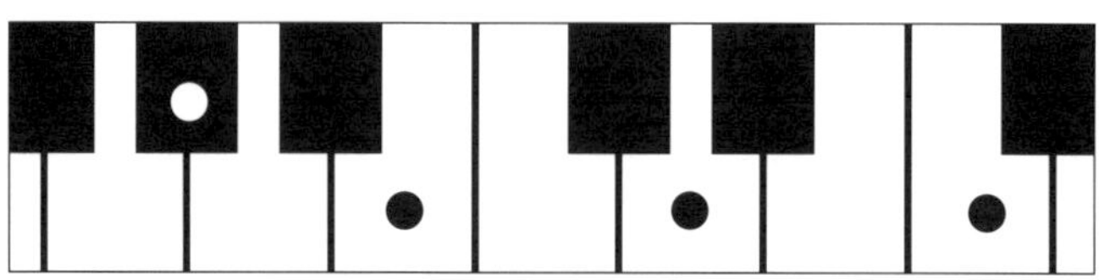

Chromatic scales

A chromatic scale is built of semitones. On the piano you simply play all the keys in order in half-tone steps. On other instruments it is not as simple. Reading from a scale book, chromatic scales seem a bewildering mass of sharps and flats. To clarify, play them while looking at the keyboard graphic below.

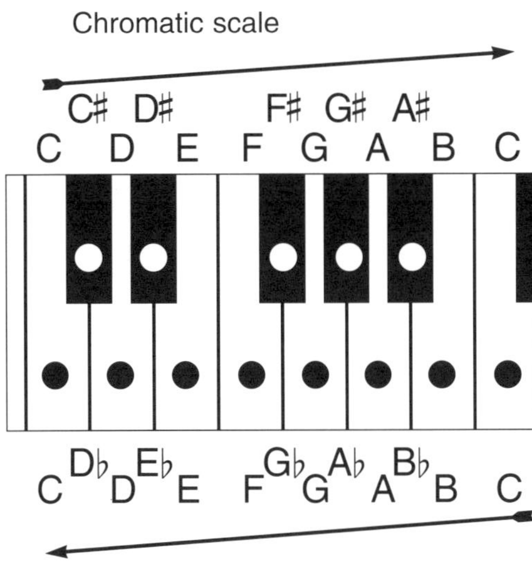

Think in terms of sharps ascending and flats descending, as scale books show. On the downward run, if the accidentals were written as sharps, you would come to F# before F. But if you think of F# as G♭ there is a flow in the order: G G♭ F rather than G F# F – the same three notes.

Break them up into bite-size bits of four or five notes at a time. If you use a scale book, cover the page with pieces of paper so that you see only a small group of notes at any time, moving the paper to extend your range until the whole scale is covered.

Whole-tone scales

Whole-tone scales consist of full tones only, therefore they have no semitones. Pianists manage these easily as they can see the patterns of black and white notes. Other instrumentalists can understand them by looking at the keyboard graphics below.

There are only two patterns. The first starts on C and uses the three black notes F# G# A#. It looks like this:

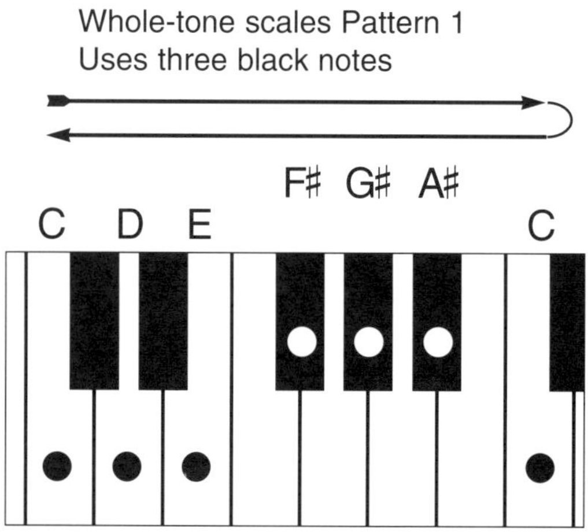

The second pattern starts on C# and uses the two black notes C# and D#.

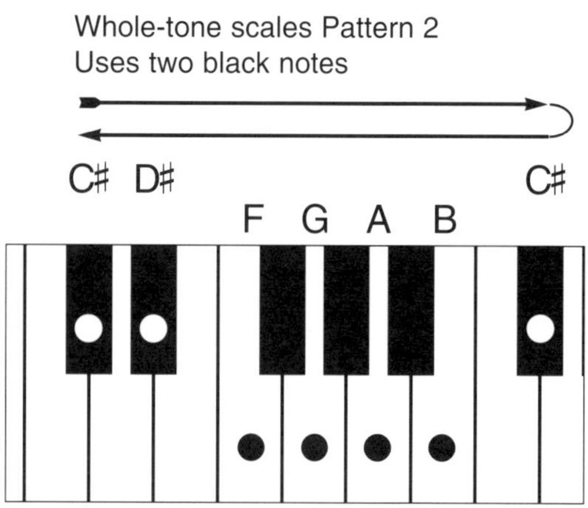

After learning these two patterns, it's a simple matter of recycling to build scales starting on different notes within each pattern.

Scales in Thirds

Scales in thirds are built in a leapfrog pattern. Start on the tonic note, jump to the third note of the scale then back to the second. Continue this pattern of jumping and returning up and down the scale.

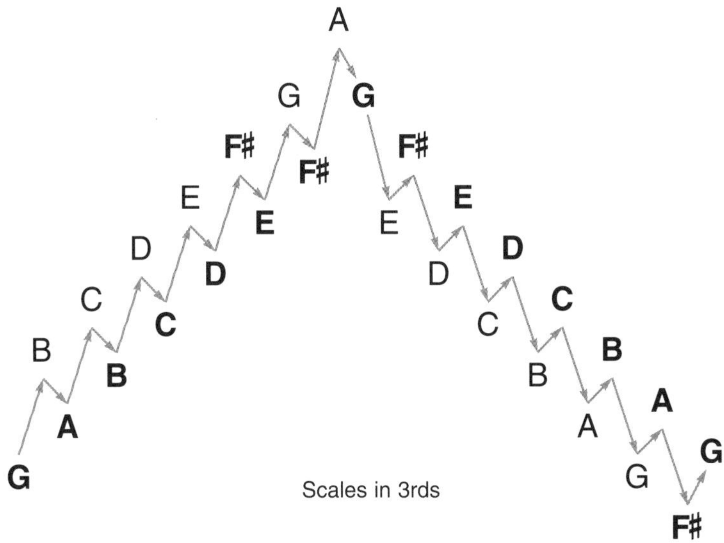

Scales in 3rds

Ways to enliven scale work

- Play the scales/arpeggios in the rhythm of that piece you are learning.
- Sing the notes of the scales as you finger them on your instrument. Better still, sing them in Solfa.
- Pianists can play three or four notes together as (discordant) block chords up the scale.
- Memorise the shapes under your hands.
- Finger in the air the shapes made by the scale patterns.

- Play in different rhythms:
  - dotteds (short-long and long-short)
  - triplets
  - groups of fives, sevens, nines
  - syncopated.
- Play trapeze-like, up and down without stopping.
- Work mainly on the tip of the iceberg.
- Start small and add a note.
- Expand ripples from the trickiest intervals.
- Start the scale on a note other than the tonic.
- Work in manageable bite-size bits, up and down: Repeat each several times, so your brain actually absorbs odd patterns or smooths fingering glitches.
- Play in half-scale chunks, called tetrachords. You will find they recycle. If you learn half a scale it is included in two or three other scales. For example, the first tetrachord of C major is the second tetrachord of F major.
- Vary with different articulations, dynamics.
- Improvise in the key after you have played the scale.

Ways to work smart with scales

Let's pause for a reality check. Is there anything more unpalatable in music (even, in life) than playing scales? Yet without fluent scale practice, there is little chance of playing that flashy piece that makes listeners' eyes widen, that passes auditions, or that hooks the prize gigs.

Reality Check: Just playing through a scale or arpeggio is not enough. Many players give up at the 'once will do' point, not realising that 'once' is not enough to cement it into the muscle memory. Scales need to be played over and over and over, day after day, week after week, if they are to be produced on demand without a blink in performance.

Let's look at sport. How many times does a top player work to finesse a stroke?

It takes three thousand repetitions of a golf swing to put it in the muscle memory, and ten thousand repetitions to cement it into the sub-conscious. If one translates that into music, that's a lot of solid practice! (Research at University of Otago School of Physical Education.)

Parrot-fashion learning may seem dated in the 21st century, but it is essential for success with music–especially with scales. Only the most committed could face three thousand repetitions, but three hundred? Thirty? Even five repetitions make an improvement. Repeat five times a week. You will surely see improvement. If you choose to lift that to seven or ten times, you will progress faster.

The High 5s for top results

Discuss with your teacher which scales, bars or passages need the High 5 treatment. That means you will need to play them five times – correctly!– on five days. If you make a mistake, go back to the beginning so you play five consecutive times. Then cross off and repeat tomorrow.

Apply the 80-20 rule

Many students complain of being overcommitted, with so many activities to fit into the days and weeks. Work smart! Maximise your results by applying the 80-20 Pareto Principle. (See internet http://www.gassner.co.il/pareto/)

Whether it's a scale, a technical study or a piece of music, identify where improvement is most needed – the 20% for example. (You can play the easy parts, right? So why waste time simply reinforcing them, possibly becoming stale? Concentrate on the most important 20%. Allocate 80% of your time to this.)

Ask yourself: which 20% of work will lead to 80% success?

For example: The scale of A harmonic minor (below) needs most work on just the top few notes. The rest is as easy as ABC. Here's the formula: 20% of the scale needs 80% of your time. 80% of results come from 20% of effort.

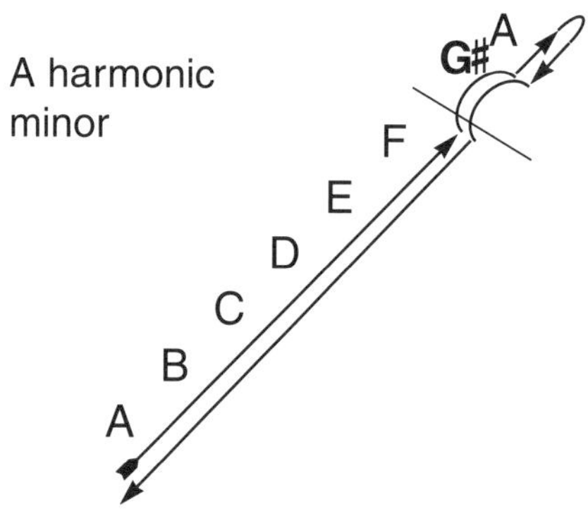

Scale-athon

Try out your skills with scales by getting together with other players of a similar standard to hold a "Scale-athon". Agree on a list of scales to be prepared, write their names on pieces of paper to be drawn from a hat. Each player starts with a kitty of jellybeans. In turn, each contestant plays the scale selected from the hat: if correct the first time, they win a jellybean; if incorrect a jellybean is forfeited. Wind up with improvisation, sight reading or a jam session.

The bottom line is that you can perform them accurately on demand while still having some fun.

With all your brilliant technique you can play just about anything.

Chapter 6

Managing teachers and parents

Few young musicians are immune from conflict with parents or teachers at some point. Were the big-names any different? Beethoven confessed that as a boy he had been "careless and rarely made to work" and that his musical education had been a bad one. Even he wept over his early music lessons and his alcoholic father, a singer, beat him. However the adult Beethoven told the piano teacher of his nephew Carl: "I beg you to keep him to his work, otherwise there is no use in his having a teacher."

Wolfgang Amadeus Mozart's father, Leopold, was such a strong-minded task-master that the adolescent Wolfgang, to assert himself against his father, went off to live in Vienna to gain some space. Once he wrote to Leopold: "As soon as people lose confidence in me, I am apt to lose confidence in myself."

Parents and teachers feed the line that their pressure and pushing is done for the good of the student, even though it might not feel like it at the time.

You might often say: "I hate it when they nag." But teachers and parents dislike nagging just as much as you loathe listening to it.

Try looking at it from their side. It's their job to guide you. If they get no reactions, zero results, what's the next move? They nag more. Surely it causes less aggro to get on and do the work than to listen to more of the same.

It could be worse. Used to be. At least the days of teachers hitting students' fingers with a ruler are passed. Victims warned of one frustrated, embittered nineteenth-century piano teacher, Adolf von Henselt: "Don't go near him; Henselt kills."

Yet a student of his contemporary Franz Liszt said: "He doesn't keep nagging but leaves you to your own conception. With a few words he gives you enough to think about for the rest of your life."

When music lessons are on a one-to-one basis the relationship between teacher and pupil is vital; this can be truly rewarding, perhaps the only opportunity some students have for interaction at a deep level with an adult other than a parent. There may be times when issues other than music stray into the lesson and a teacher can provide a listening ear for problems. Many teachers become role models, amateur psychologists, counsellors, friends.

Of course, as with all relationships, there may be a personality clash. First, give the teacher a fair trial and sufficient time to get used to each others' quirks. If, after a few months you really feel uncomfortable with the relationship, calmly suggest incompatibility to your parent. Bad-mouthing the teacher only muddies the issue. All such relationships are two-way affairs.

A change of teacher can be unsettling. Perhaps you were very happy with a former teacher, who, for whatever reason, was unable to continue lessons. It may be hard to settle down to a new teacher's methods but resist the tendency to compare. Give it time. Keep an open mind. A different slant and a change of pace often prove refreshing.

Few other activities require the degree of commitment and regular work that music does. We have to invest time and energy to reap rewards; music requires

- Write biog for Carnegie Hall debut concert
- Write parody of teacher's program biog
- Unpack and pack instrument veeery slooowly
- Search for really high notes that don't exist on your instrument

active not passive involvement. Only then will we meet music's challenges and feel the joy of achievement.

Students may think: "My teacher doesn't seem to realise that I have lots else in my life (sport, assignments, part-time job) and music is just a small part of my routine." If so, initiate a discussion early in each semester to update on new pressures in your timetable – before they reach aggression point.

Sometimes a teacher's enthusiasm to help you to shine can translate as pressure. As it is their job to tell you how to "get better" they may not realise that you seem to only hear the bad news; that you need the encouragement of some congratulation and good reports. The performing arts tend to be the realm of perfectionists.

If you have made a genuine, consistent effort which appears to be unrewarded and you feel overwhelmed by comments, level with them. They may not realise how their efforts to stretch and challenge your excellent talent have been received. Give them a chance to respond to your feedback before deciding it may be time for a change.

Perhaps the choice of material is not to your taste? Be aware that we all need finger work-outs to develop a foundation. If you would like to add to the program extra pieces that are more to your style try these lines:

"I was browsing in a shop and found this great book; d'you think I could manage this with a bit of work?" (Teachers are suckers for the W-Word.)

Or: "A friend lent me this book and, as well as the pieces you set, I prepared this extra one."

Your teacher will be very impressed by your initiative and probably will set more similar pieces. If they think it an ambitious leap, ask "What work do I need to do to play it?"

Parental involvement

Teachers often note that parents who take an active interest in their children's progress breed the more competent musicians. Of

Excuses, excuses…

- It's my mother's fault. She didn't make me practise this week, she only reminded me
- Dad can't afford to pay the bill, so I supposed we'd stopped
- You said I had talent, so I don't need to practise
- Mum ran out of change to pay me
- You gave me a big sticker last week
- Mum's sick and my tuba has gone out in sympathy
- You said we were going to work on theory this week
- I thought my lesson wasn't until Friday
- My friend slammed my finger in the door
- Grandma came to stay
- If you practise too much you get stale and get worse
- I had lots of projects
- Dad won't let me play 'cause the piano is in the TV room
- There's a westerly wind blowing and I've had asthma

course, there are parents and there are parents. Some manage to sit in on lessons without muttered interruptions, or telling the teachers the story of their own musical life. Or spilling embarrassing stories about you.

Parents may be tolerated in lessons, but only if both teacher and pupil are comfortable and positive about it. Even body language of parents engrossed in the newspaper can be inhibiting. If either student or teacher feels intimidated, threatened, harassed or just overwhelmed by parental zeal, they can suggest the parent wait outside.

The trouble is, they are the ones paying. So it is understandable they want to get their money's worth. But they should realise progress can be inhibited by their well-meaning presence. Drop a hint to your teacher, who might use a tactful phrase like "I think your child will progress faster if you are not in the room."

Parents from hell

At home parents can be such help – reminding you of the lovely studies you forgot to bring home from the lesson. Or finding the scale book hidden under the couch.

But when it comes to exams and competitions they can be more of a hindrance than a help. A common complaint is: "My parents get so uptight about each performance."

Some parents from hell spread tension like a virus. It's enough hassle managing the performance without a parent drama as well.

To be fair, the sheer effort of organising extra lessons, accompanists, photocopies for the adjudicator and finding strange venues is enough to frazzle the most level-headed parent. However, if you feel that your parents create excess stress, try this line:

"I think I will manage this better if you give me space to focus." As you pass them the newspaper and wave them towards the foyer.

When they expect too much

"My parents seem to think I'm going to be a musical prodigy. I just want to be a computer programmer."

Warn them of the dangers of burn-out. Quote the pianist Franz Liszt: "You cannot imagine how it spoils one to have been a child prodigy." This megastar became "weary of the public, weary of their cheap applause." For the last 40 years of his life he gave only charity concerts.

Who is this for?

Parents want their kids to have wonderful opportunities that they missed themselves. Fine. Except if yours are trying to realise their own dreams through you. If so, perhaps they could take lessons also. Offer to lend them the instrument when you're busy with homework. Tell them that it is never too late, that it's rubbish you have to start music lessons from the cradle. What they lack in finger dexterity can be balanced by their maturity and motivation. Turn the tables; bribe them to practise!

Parents and prodigies

So you think you've got problems with your parents? Legend has it that when Toscanini, the famous conductor, was a boy, he was locked in the room to practise. So what could he do about going to the toilet? He had to widdle in his cello.

Poor pianist Josef Hofman, aged 10, asked plaintively "What do they want to make a little boy like me work so hard for? I am not able to do it" – meaning 52 concerts in 10 weeks! The New York

Society for the Prevention of Cruelty to Children insisted on a medical examination which found signs of "mental derangement". A wealthy philanthropist paid the father to keep Josef off the stage until he was 18.

Be glad you don't have the parents of composer Isaac Albeniz. A piano prodigy at four, he was dragged along to perform dressed as a French musketeer, rapier and all. Not surprisingly, he ran away from home and became a street kid. Aged 12, he stowed away on a ship bound for Puerto Rico and supported himself by playing in saloons and on a lone recital tour from Cuba to San Francisco.

See, it could be worse.

However, positive parental involvement helps students of all instruments. Their encouragement is particularly valuable with students of the stringed instruments, where initial results are slow and it may take some time to produce a singing, well-tuned tone.

Parental involvement is central to the Suzuki Method, founded by world renowned educator, Dr Shinichi Suzuki. His "mother tongue" concept is that children effortlessly and enthusiastically pick up language, a word at a time, by listening to their parents. Observing that all children are capable of learning their native language without formal lessons, he concluded that children have a great potential for learning if given the correct environment. "All children everywhere," says Dr Suzuki in his book *Nurtured by Love*, "are brought up by a perfect educational method – their mother tongue. Why not apply this to other faculties?" The parent is the cornerstone of the Suzuki triangle of teacher, student and parent, and learns the instrument along with the child. He says that "parents who understand children make fine teachers ... an unlimited amount of ability can develop when parent and child are having fun together."

Dr Suzuki says that in the early stages (children are encouraged to begin at three or four years of age) practice should be "three minutes, ten times a day with love."

Anyone can face three minutes' practice at a time, as long as they love their instrument.

Chapter 7

The right instrument for you

Music students are frequently seen by their parents as being lazy when they don't practise as much as they think they should. But there are often genuine reasons why some students cannot face serious, lengthy and focused work.

Perhaps the problem is not mere lack of motivation. They might simply be incompatible with the instrument chosen. Many abandoned instruments cultivate mould and dust under beds because they were just not suited to their owners.

Size matters

Frustrations can be caused when instruments built for adult-sized hands are put into young children's small fingers. A youngster who lacks fine motor coordination may struggle with a violin but manage a saxophone more easily. But imagine the difficulties a small child would have with a baritone saxophone that is very nearly bigger than him. The young saxophonist is advised to begin with the alto instrument rather than tenor or baritone. A small trumpeter can start with a cornet, which, being conical, is compact. The weight and finger or arm stretch of tuba, trombone and bassoon are daunting and uncomfortable to smaller physiques. Or a young girl's clarinet may frequently squeak because her thin fingers can barely cover the holes. She would manage much better with the covered holes found on flutes and saxophones.

Playing an incompatible instrument can cause tension leading to fatigue, frustration and possibly repetitive strain injury. Tests are available through some music shops and schools to assess a student's suitability to the instrument of choice. Discuss with your teacher.

Many factors come into the equation – the varying rates of

physical development, maturity, coordination and concentration. Of course, if a student really loves a particular instrument and its sound, most incompatibilities can be overcome.

Many well-intentioned parents begin their children's music lessons before coordination and concentration skills are sufficiently mature. This may frustrate and cause negative impressions – "Oh, I'm not musical; I gave up the trombone in primary school". On the other hand, early musical education is to be encouraged. Scientific studies show that music training in the first decades of a child's life increases aural acuity and intelligence, as music uses both right and left hemispheres of the brain (see Chapter 9).

Early starters

The secret is to choose carefully which form of music is undertaken. Singing, movement and clapping games are ideal from

toddler stages. Various music education systems such as Kodaly, Dalcroze, Forte, Encore and Yamaha are invaluable precursors to playing an instrument as they develop aural, pitch, rhythmic and coordination skills.

Keyboard and stringed instruments are probably the only ones which benefit from a very young commencement age. The issues of size, finger stretch and weight for young violinists are solved by giving them smaller instruments appropriate to their age – eighth or even sixteenth size violins and celli are available. A three quarter-size guitar is available for young guitarists.

Don't overlook the human voice as a wonderful instrument; it is free, light and easily transported, unlike the double bass or tuba. It can be utilised from babyhood on, develops remarkably with use and provides invaluable development for other future instrumental studies. Repertoire is broad, catering to all tastes and styles.

Physical points

Given that young people develop at varying rates, it is important to not take generalisations too seriously. However, the following points are a reasonable rule of thumb:

Good coordination is required to do justice to the string family. As noted in the previous chapter, Dr Suzuki advocates starting stringed instruments as young as three or four; however, some teachers and parents prefer the benefit of a few years' maturity and schools recommend Year 3. Because the viola and double bass require wider hand stretching, it is wise to wait until they may be taken up as a second instrument. As cello and bass are supported on the ground, the weight issue is negligible.

Most children manage wood-wind instruments from around Year 5 (approximately aged 10). It is wise to wait a few years, even until high school, before taking up instruments such as the bassoon, oboe, tuba or euphonium – but there are always exceptions of young players who cope splendidly.

Lighter high brass instruments are usually managed without strain from about nine to 10 years of age. The trombone can be managed by Year 5 students if they are reasonably well built.

Because of weight, it is advisable to begin with either the tenor trombone or the baritone (three-valve). The F trigger or bass instruments should not be considered until more advanced. Younger players may have difficulty reaching the sixth and seventh positions on the B♭ tenor trombone.

With lower brass, younger players aged around 10 can begin with single horn or tuba as they are simpler and lighter than the double instruments. The tuba and and all brass in general require solid physical development and more air than for many instruments.

All brass and woodwind instruments require well formed dental structure, and it is advisable to begin lessons only when the front adult teeth have stabilised. Playing with gaps caused by lost baby teeth can be tricky.

Orthodontic work also may cause discomfort at times but most wind and brass players manage to survive these torrid times. Teachers will suggest strategies to compensate.

Personality

Music offers a wide palette of sounds and colours, and people respond uniquely to each. Bright or dark? Rich and resonant or subtle, dulcet?

Instruments have their own personalities as well as sounds and, if they are matched to the players' personalities, practice and performance are easier. Once we discover which instrument suits our personality, motivation is a cinch. Some people need scope for dramatic expression, others revel in flashy virtuosity; another may prefer a soothing or dark, reflective sound.

Many players are unconsciously drawn to a certain range or timbre. Girls may identify with the flute as its range corresponds to their voices. Similarly, adolescent boys are drawn to the lower brass.

Some musicians prefer to be team-players in the string section, other up-front individuals thrive as wind or brass principals. While some enjoy the challenge of pitching each note individually (strings, trombone), others prefer the security of knowing that where they put their finger down produces the exact note (keyboard, woodwind). Then there are those who thrive on the mental stretch of a transposing instrument (French horn, clarinet, trumpet).

Hyperactive youngsters are likely to enjoy the challenge of managing multiple instruments in the percussion section, channelling their energy into flourishing drumsticks or crashing cymbals. Physical stamina and mental energy are needed. Percussionists are the only orchestral players who stand and move around from one instrument to another – a boon for quick-witted, bright, "butterfly" fidgeting personalities. Percussion offers a variety of instruments, tuned and untuned, so can suit those of varying aural ability. Tuned instruments like timpani need an acute ear, as opposed to keyboard forms which are already tuned. Younger players can start side-drum from around eight years, but the coordination necessary for drum-kit and tuned percussion develops around the early teens.

The violin's challenging technique often appeals to conscientious perfectionists, perhaps the first child in a family, who may have more available time with a parent. Violists face other issues, such as a larger finger stretch and heavier weight on the shoulder but this is compensated by generally easier orchestral parts and fewer solos. They, and double bass players, tend to be reliable, supportive team players. The cello offers players the choice of generally comfortable, easy harmonic bass lines, or, for the star players, solos played with rich, dark and expressive tone.

Flautists may be attracted to their instrument's soft sound, but it also offers brilliant agility. Oboists have a tendency to be soulful, expressive personalities, especially evident when they play the related cor anglais. The bassoon's rather comic sound attracts those with a strong sense of humour, the comedians of the orchestra. The clarinet's wide range of timbre and styles (jazz, marching bands, as well as orchestral) gives scope for both the reflective and artistic but also the outgoing and sociable so they often tend to be broad interest lateral thinkers.

Saxophones are magnets for versatile and outgoing people, – the "cool dudes". Similarly, the guitar is a popular instrument especially amongst teenage boys, with a rock band being something of a rite of passage. Yet the classical guitar also offers wide scope for the reflective, interpretative personalities.

Trumpeters – as do most brass players – tend to have positive, outgoing personalities, forthright and confident. Bright all-rounders, but also reflective people are attracted to the trombone's mellow tone. The horn's rich timbre suits deep thinkers, introverts and more intense personalities.

Keyboard instruments offer a wide range of register, harmonic potential and styles with ample scope for all personalities.

Relative costs for beginner instruments

It is difficult to quantify costs as the quality of an instrument can cause huge variables. However, for beginner instruments, the following points may be made:

- Stringed instruments will probably require periodic size upgrades from eighth to quarter to half and on to three-quarter and full.

Excuses, excuses...

- I can't take my bari sax home because I ride a bike.
- I might get repetitive strain injury.
- I took my instrument apart and couldn't get it back together.
- My instrument needs fixing.
- Where did you say the repair shop is?
- Our puppy chewed through the bow-hairs.
- I decided I'd rather play saxophone.
- I'm allergic to the reed – playing makes me itch.

- Most woodwind beginner instruments fall in the "average" price bracket, with the saxophone, oboe and bassoon higher than clarinet or flute.
- The cornet and trumpet tend to be less expensive than the horn, trombone, euphonium or tuba.
- Guitars range from relatively inexpensive to higher costs.

Aural acuity

Playing of certain instruments (the stringed family, trombone, horn) is considered to need strong aural perception in order to pitch each note individually. However, other instrumentalists need to maintain vigilant listening skills also and should not become complacent because fingerings imply that their notes will be produced – what you press is what you get.

General pointers

The saxophone fingering is similar to the recorder. The beginner range of the flute corresponds with girls' singing voices, the clarinet with that of young boys.

Brass instruments are popular with both boys and girls. A teacher can advise regarding choice of high brass (cornet, trumpet, horn) or low brass (trombone, euphonium, baritone, tuba). The trombone's slide technique may take a little longer to master than the valve technique of other brass. The trombone is a versatile instrument, found in most ensembles. Players intend to take examinations will need to handle trombone clefs and horn, trumpet and clarinet transposition.

Further reading: *The Right Instrument for your Child; a practical guide for parents and teachers* by A. Ben-Tovin and D. Boyd (Gollancz, London) and *The Musical Temperament; Psychology and Personality of Musicians* by Anthony E. Kemp (OUP. 1996).

If your instrument makes you sick

Complaints like "my instrument is such poor quality, it gives me a headache to play it" or "I'll need a better one if I'm going to work harder" may seem mere excuses unless approached the right way. A teacher's opinion can clarify this for parents.

Certainly, poor quality equipment can make practice unpleasant, even uncomfortable. But there is a better chance that your parents will put their hard-earned money into an upgrade if you have shown yourself motivated and keen. If you rarely play, why should they pay? Rightly, they should first expect to see serious effort.

Parents may think you are fickle if you frequently ask to change instruments, arguing "I think I'd do better with a different instrument." Maybe you might. But you do need to give this one sufficient time to reap results and satisfaction before giving up. Music isn't a quick-fix game. If you constantly shilly-shally, your parents will hardly face more outlay of costs.

Perhaps you genuinely want to learn another instrument but you are stuck with your present one. After all, once you are proficient with one instrument, the next may be relatively easy. Consider saving your own money to rent your preferred instrument from a shop; or discuss with your school if you could borrow one over the holidays to experiment. It is wise to have some lessons to set correct foundations and avoid discouragement.

Many players develop a close friendship with their instruments, enjoying the opportunity to express themselves, their thoughts and emotions through their playing. English cellist Jacqueline du Pré as a child was "very introverted and desperately shy … I loved the fact that one could be so private with the cello and communicate one's innermost thoughts to it. It became a person, you could even say a love."

Choose an instrument that most appeals to you. It will become a friend rather than foe, a pleasure to spend time with. Then practice will not be a dirty word.

Chapter 8

Exams, recitals, competitions

You have put in the hard work with practice – all those scales and playing your pieces over and over. Now comes the real test. What will others – your examiner, your audience at a public performance or the person who auditions you – think? Let us see the results of all your hard work.

Time your arrival at a peak

Timing is essential. Sometimes we are puzzled that, in spite of enormous efforts, progress on a work goes backwards. If we labour over a piece for months on end, it may become tired and stale, resisting all efforts. Discuss with your teacher whether it has already reached and passed its peak. Is there time to let it rest for a few weeks before the performance? In dire circumstances, you and your teacher may decide to beat a tactical retreat. Choose a fresh piece with a new set of challenges. In the meantime, you will be refreshed by playing another piece. You will be surprised how the staleness falls away when you return to the first piece.

Success with recitals and exams

Pitfalls are lessened if you know the music thoroughly – both your part and, equally importantly, the accompaniment. Listen to recordings and live performances of the work. Practise from the full score so you can see how the parts interlock.

Think before the first rehearsal: Where would you need an emergency breath in performance? Can you manage it all in one breath? (Or, for string players, a different bowing?) What works easily at home may be less comfortable in performance

Where is each phrase heading? It's got to have a direction! If you just mooch through the piece it will be dead boring.

Pre-performance tips:

- Play dummy-runs to Mum, Dad, Grandma and the budgie to get used to an audience. Or offer to play for the local kindergarten, retirement village or church.
- Practise stage presentation and body work. If possible, play through in the auditorium to get used to the acoustics and balance, and to projecting in a larger space. Bring a friend or teacher along to give feedback.
- Check dress requirement well before and iron your clothes early to avoid last-minute mishaps. Perform the piece through in your concert gear to get the feel of it.
- Prepare all equipment, including spare strings, reeds, repair kit.
- Big picture work: Get used to playing the entire piece without stopping, no matter what happens.
- Building stamina: Play the whole piece through five times in a row without stopping. (But note any mishaps which recur. Clarify them with slow detailed work – see Chapter 3.)
- Mental Visualisation: Sit quietly with the score and sing through the part. Visualise yourself walking confidently on stage, bowing, playing with ease, acknowledging the applause. See yourself with diary open, trying to find time for a repeat performance!

Rehearsal with your accompanist

A supportive accompanist can be an enormous boost to your own confidence in performance. It is important to spend sufficient time together, not just to ensure technical agreement but also to build a rapport. Treat your accompanist with consideration and courtesy; mutual respect goes a long way.

Before your rehearsal:

- Pencil into the piano score any cuts, breath marks, tempo changes, dynamics. This enables the pianist to follow you smoothly, without having to stop and check that you meant what you played.
- Listen to a recording of the work so you know how the intro, the rest bars, all those tricky entries should fit. If possible, play them on the piano.
- Pencil cues into your own part. Even a sketchy rhythmic skeleton makes a great security blanket when you're unsure of entries.
- Check with your teacher that your rhythm is secure. Practise with a metronome. Consider any tempo changes.
- Write clearly all details of the performance venue, date and time on a piece of paper and attach it to the score.
- Check payment for your pianist and have the money ready after the show.
- Triple-check that you take all required music to the rehearsal. Accompanists tell horror stories of having to make up sketchy chords after a player arrives empty handed and says blankly, "Oh, do you need music?"
- Even better, deliver the music to accompanists several weeks before the first rehearsal, so they can work out page turns, tricky fingerings and difficult passages.
- Practise giving up-beats in the tempo you really mean, remembering that in performance the adrenal rush may cause your pulse to race.

At the rehearsal:

Before starting, silently sing the opening phrase so that you establish the speed at which you are comfortable. Or play a few bars to demonstrate your tempo. However, experienced pianists are quick to catch your tempo as long as you give clear signals, with uncluttered body language. Beware of giving mixed signals, like a toe which taps an unconscious cross-rhythm.

Most accompanists can pick up a tempo from the speed of wind players' and singers' breath intakes, so be sure to breathe in the tempo.

Angle yourself so you have good eye contact with each other. Look at your accompanist. Then back at the music. Meaningful eye-contact is very important.

The performance

Your first phrase has to be a beauty, poised and confident. This will be possible only if you have prepared properly and considered issues like the following:

- **Where am I heading?** Know where each phrase leads.
- **Where will I breathe/bow?** Have plenty of scope for breaths, so there will be no unexpected pressure.

Take your time before starting to perform

Before playing a note, make eye contact with pianist. Nod. Look back at the music.

This is your time, don't let the sight of a busily writing examiner, juror or a shuffling audience hassle you into starting before you are ready. These very important few seconds enable you to gather poise as you mentally sing the first phrase or two to stabilise the tempo.

First impressions count

Look like you know what you're doing, where you're going. If the first opening phrase is poised and secure your morale will soar.

You can live down a bad first impression, but it's a lot easier to build on a strong beginning. Thorough rehearsal with the accompanist will give you both confidence if you come unstuck from your pianist mid-piece, which can happen to even the most experienced players.

If you make a mistake, keep going rhythmically and rely on the accompanist to find you. If you wander back to pick up that lost note or beat, you may both grope for each other in the frightening

fog of no-man's land. Pianists soon learn to jump a beat, bar or line without the slightest flicker to give the show away – after all the solo line is written in their score. They accept that it is their role to reconnoitre, yours to lead. Trust your accompanist.

If your brain has been correctly programmed you do not need to fear a few moments' panic in an exam or a performance. Let your brain go into auto-drive. Your fingers will move automatically until the fog in your mind clears. Therein lies confidence!

How to impress the examiner, adjudicator or auditioner

- Play out with a big, positive tone. Even if the first dynamic is marked pianissimo, notch it higher. Remember, first impressions count. You don't want them to think you a wimp.
- Exaggerate all dynamics. Just as a soapie actor over-plays all emotions, so too you should intensify all expression. Triple it. This simple quick-fix makes the examiner or adjudicator think; "Aha, musical!" Often we may act a dynamic with our body language, but less comes out in the actual sound.
- Act poised. Even if you are a quivering mess. Pretend. Body language which says "I am the greatest" might just bluff yourself as well as the listeners.

Examinations

Exams are different to recitals, competitions and auditions. They require a wider range of preparations. As well as requiring competent presentation of the pieces, you also have to be ready for the things the examiner will throw at you – scales, arpeggios, exercises, sight reading, aural tests and general knowledge. If you are not prepared for all of these aspects your grading will suffer.

The other issue is that an examination is an unnatural performance situation. You are without the empathy of the audience's response and painfully conscious of the examiners' close presence in a small studio and their incessant writing. In the tension of this situation you might assume that they are scribbling a negative running commentary on your performance. But they might well be complimenting your musicianship rather than noting your every mistake.

We have seen in Chapter 3 the importance of preparation. So of course we are thoroughly prepared for examinations. Our scales zoom up and down without a hiccup, never a whisker of hesitation or wrong notes. We have practised aural tests for months and our pieces are note-perfect, sensitively and musically phrased.

The warm-up

Those crucial minutes in the warm-up room may spell the difference between poise and fluster inside the exam room. It is essential to build confidence with a steady, accurate and clear warm-up before facing the examiner. If we rip through the most daunting, tricky passage at break-neck speed, it may do more damage than good. We risk falling into pot-holes of mistakes, the same ones over and over. Oops, keep going, splat, zoom, kerplunk, fizzle out. To walk into the exam room knowing that we have just turned the etude into tangled spaghetti is hardly confidence-building.

Play that difficult passage if you will, but at half-speed. Better still, warm up with slow scales, long notes (especially for singers, strings, wind and brass players) and calming slow, deep breaths. Stretching exercises and deep yawns help to release tension.

Accompaniment

It is absolutely essential to rehearse together before the examination, as ensemble work is an important aspect. The examiner soon guesses if a candidate and accompanist meet for the first time in the exam room. Hesitant openings, disagreements over tempo changes and general insecurity give this away. It is important to practise giving clear upbeats.

Dynamics

Many pieces open with a soft dynamic. A positive opening is

important to the listener and increases the player's confidence. Arrest the examiner's attention with a full, positive sound, not a small, mousy one. If it is marked piano, think of a soft white rabbit instead of a mouse and bump up the dynamic to mezzo-forte.

Bluff yourself as well as the examiner by playing out with a big, bold sound and with a wide range of dynamics and colour. Even if the composer marked little interest into the piece, add your own ideas. Be adventurous and imaginative. Why not make it your goal to turn that study which you thought was so boring into an interesting piece? Why not play the scales with a full, positive tone? Examiners love such enterprise.

Tuning

Often when nervous, it is difficult to hear tuning, as panic seems to clog our ears. Practise tuning to the piano over several rehearsals. If unsure whether the note is sharp or flat, listen to the "beats". Try humming quietly the piano note you heard. Ask the pianist to play a D minor chord, instead of just A. If you are really unsure, suggest before the exam that the pianist raise or lower an eyebrow.

Aural tests

Similarly, confusion can result from nerves and panic. This is minimised if aural tests have been practised for a few minutes each lesson over the past months, rather than in a burst at the end of the last lesson. Do not hesitate to ask the examiner to play the tests an octave lower if this helps lower voices. When recognising intervals, those who audibly sing and count up are often out, usually by one interval, showing a flaw in their method. It is better to learn to recognise the intervals, perhaps linking them to familiar songs.

General knowledge

It is sad that so many players miss the point of a piece by neglecting to read and understand its title. A Pastorale, Burlesque, Badinerie, Reverie, Elegie, Humoreske, Aria, Nocturne, Fughetta, Sicilienne, Carol, or Idyll all give important clues to the moods and styles to be played. Many players miss the fun of a piece, perhaps not expecting to play a Burlesque really "over the top". Knowing that the word means, in common usage, to take the micky out of someone or something allows the player to let loose. The dictionary defines burlesque as: "imitate for purpose of deriding or amusing … caricature, parody, variety show frequently featuring comic strip-tease". And a Badinerie is a game, a trifle, a dancelike piece that's comical, a bit of a joke. How can you play a piece really well if you don't know its basic meaning?

Analysis of the piece allows the player to understand its structure, how the composer crafted it. It helps our appreciation and interpretation to know about the composers and their place in the perspective of history, of what other events were happening at the time, which composers came before to influence them.

Scales

Examiners love candidates who play fluent, correct scales. Examiners, always on a tight schedule, are reluctant to give second or third tries at scales to someone who never did know the right notes anyway. The examiner is not impressed by the candidate who detours around potholes and turns a three octave scale, which should contain forty-three notes, into an obstacle race of seventy-six, collapsing on the leading note instead of the tonic. This Snakes and Ladders game, which can take a whole minute of the time allotted, is not appreciated by examiners.

> **Hot tip!**
>
> *EXAMINERS LOVE CANDIDATES WHO PLAY FLUENT, CORRECT SCALES*

Examiners can be less than sympathetic to candidates who have never really come to grips with the difference between major and minor scales, let alone between harmonic and melodic ones. This can be the moment of truth for the student who has put the minor scales in the too-hard basket.

Examiners become adept at sensing whether the scale was incorrect because of nerves, or because it was never known in the first place. A big give-away is that the candidate invariably drops the volume when attempting a scale that's not secure. Combat this by playing those tricky scales louder and slower … for don't we all rush when unsure?

Examiners prefer candidates to take a few seconds to think before launching into a scale, than to spend half a minute trying this note, then that, then going back to the beginning for another ill-fated try. So, when your mind becomes a blank, stop. Think for five seconds. Play clearly, slowly and with conviction and you might win over the examiner! Think of key signatures, don't fly off into the fog on a wing and a prayer.

Equipment

Always organise any equipment well before the examination. String players should carry extra strings. Don't forget shoulder-rests, rosin, or other equipment. Keep a screwdriver in wind or brass instrument cases. Wind-players should take their pull-through or swab into the examination room; it is acceptable to take a few moments to clean out between longer pieces. Pianists should not hesitate to adjust the piano stool to a comfortable height, or to ask for another chair. Reed-players should start "blowing-in" reeds weeks beforehand to have several spare ones in case your tried and trusty reed packs it in.

General points

Confidence comes from being well prepared. Pre-examination organisation increases poise. Check the current syllabus well before the exam rather than run the risk of being downgraded because you presented inappropriate or insufficient pieces.

Hot tip!

PREPARATION CREATES CONFIDENCE

Before entering the exam room check you have all music and equipment. A rush back to the waiting room will make you flustered and breathless.

If during your exam you need a drink of water, ask for it (preferably bring your water bottle). A drink between pieces helps calm you and clear your head. Before playing, use a few moments to take in details of key signature, dynamics and rhythm of your music, especially for sight reading tests. If you did not hear directions clearly, ask the examiner to repeat them. Take a deep breath, think positively, play beautifully ... and you won't need to rely on luck.

A few stumbles or slips do not spell major doom. If you make a mistake keep going. Play out with big beautiful sound and focus on expressing your strengths. Good musicianship, expressive tone and conviction can overcome a few glitches and leave the examiner with a positive impression.

Hot tip!

A FEW SLIPS AND STUMBLES DON'T SPELL MAJOR DOOM

Examiners want the candidate to feel comfortable and do well. They don't enjoy failing them. They will give you every chance that time permits to do as well as you are able. Examiners try to encourage talent and acknowledge hard work as a well as fulfil their obligation to note areas for improvement.

Towards being a musician

Examinations, auditions, recitals and competitions are milestones along the path to musical fulfilment at whichever level you aspire, from music for pleasure and recreation to a professional career somewhere in the spectrum from classical to rock.

Chapter 9

Enjoy your music

It is unfortunate that most media attention given to young people focuses on negatives: the street kids, drug addicts, juvenile crime. What a pity that television, radio and print media rarely give space to highlight the achievements of a youth orchestra's international tour, a school musical featuring hugely talented kids, a film clip or a stunning rock band performing their own compositions.

The truth is that our schools, universities and suburbs are teeming with creative, talented and hard-working young people. I see many while teaching, examining and adjudicating. A day of competitions or examinations gives a series of short snapshots in sound. I come away from such days convinced that none of the youngsters who performed will become juvenile delinquents. Even the ones whose scales and arpeggios were obviously neglected, even the few who fail.

Candidates, whatever results they receive, have learned much even before they present in the exam room. They have applied a considerable breadth of concentration to prepare their program in its various facets across a wide spectrum (technical work as well as pieces, a study of the general knowledge, analysis of the structures and keys of the pieces).

They have developed listening skills through aural tests. Even more challenging, they have faced and overcome to some small or large extent their shyness, even horror, of having to sing in public!

The whole process of preparing an exam program, seeing it through its stages of development and consistent work to the culmination of a performance teaches perseverance, delivery and focus.

Working with an accompanist involves teamwork, give and take and listening skills. They must develop the confidence to indicate through body language and eye contact clear signals to a pianist who is often a professional, a teacher, an adult – and thus considered a superior in their eyes.

Before competing in an eisteddfod candidates have been coached by their teachers in the niceties of stage presentation. Much as they may feel a nerd at being forced to bow before and after playing, they certainly look more professional as a result. They learn to maintain a positive face even through fiascoes and to restrain their disappointment over mishaps until safely backstage.

Then there is the planning and maintaining of the practice routine, the satisfaction of seeing improvement which increases a positive self-esteem. Even if they did not win the first prize or gain top results, they deserve credit for they saw the program through to completion.

Candidates are encouraged to play out with positive projection and a wide range of dynamics. They have opportunities to express themselves in sound, mood and various styles. This may involve for many a therapeutic outlet for their tensions, aggressions and depressions.

The presentation skills required for any performance will develop confidence for positive handling of future job interviews, delivery of oral presentations, conference papers or seminars.

The performing arts are the breeding ground for exceptional young people who are disciplined, motivated and self-reliant.

Music is a brain tonic

Let's get technical for a while. Scientific studies have proved that playing music from an early age increases intelligence.

This research was summed up in a speech to the American Congress by Dr Norman Weinberger, a professor in Neurobiology and Behaviour at the University of California and the executive director of the International Foundation for Music Research. In it he said: "Music education, particularly learning to play an instrument, has been found to have many benefits on cognitive development … Music performance provides a complete mind/brain 'workout'. This workout should facilitate inter-communications between cells by strengthening synapses (the connections between brain cells) thus improving brain function. This could explain increased creativity in general. It could explain transfer effects from music to other academic subjects, because if brain circuits concerned with mathematical computation, for instance, are strengthened by music education, then they would be more effective during other tasks or situations requiring such mental activities." He said that regularly playing music not only strengthens these synapses, but brain activity can actually produce new synapses. In other words, playing music makes you more brainy!

> **Hot tip!**
>
> *PLAYING MUSIC MAKES YOU BRAINY*

Weinberger cited how music engages all major components of the human brain/mind: the sensory and perceptual, the cognitive, the "planning movements" (for example, organising a sequence of muscle actions), motor (fine muscles and gross muscle coordination), feedback/evaluation (that is, hearing if one has played the correct notes), motivational, learning and memory. Also, music performance is the one activity which involves both hemispheres of the brain. (Read his speech at: http://www.amc-music.com/musicmaking/policy/weinberger.htm)

Other research shows that music study in the first decade or so of life strengthens the brain, when, says American musician and author Don Campbell, "the *corpus callosum*, the bridge between the left and right sides of the brain, completes its development, allowing both hemispheres to respond to an event simultaneously." In his book *The Mozart Effect; Tapping the power of music to heal the body, strengthen the mind and unlock the creative spirit* (Avon Books, New York, and Hodder and Stoughton), he states: "Recent studies have found that the *corpus callosum* of musicians is thicker and more fully developed than in other people, reinforcing the idea that music enlarges existing neural pathways and stimulated learning and creativity. The *planum temporale*, located in the temporal lobe of the cortex, is also more pronounced in musicians."

It has long been accepted that music education benefits young people by teaching social and group interaction and transfers skills into language and mathematics. Many professionals in top fields like medicine are proficient musicians; doctors in countries including Germany and Australia regularly join together to form their own orchestra. Dr Weinberger says that music significantly enhances spatial intelligence, the capacity responsible for accurate perception of the visual world, the ability to recognise patterns, and higher brain functions underlying competency in such areas as complex mathematics, computer skills, the sciences, architecture, map reading, and chess.

Are all types of music beneficial to the brain? Studies cited by Campbell show that our brains respond to order as is found in Classical and Baroque music. Mozart's music has been found to be particularly effective. Dr Alfred Tomatis, the French trailblazer in this field of research, describes Mozart's music as having "an effect, an impact, which the others do not have." Tomatis says: "Exception among exceptions, he has a liberating, curative, I would even say healing power." Scientists assert that Mozart's music "may 'warm-up' the brain" and that listening to Mozart helps "organise" the firing patterns of neurons in the cerebral cortex and improve concentration. Further websites prove the scientific benefits of music: http://www.amc-music.com/musicmaking/thebrain.htm and http://www.edu-cyberpg.com/music/musicsmart2.html

Practice is *not* a dirty word

Practice surely ceases to be a "dirty word" when we realise the sheer pleasure that is available at our fingertips as we open a fresh music score and begin a journey of exploration through its harmonies.

We are fortunate to have the opportunity to develop our ability and to enjoy the wonderful wide range of music repertoire available.

Truly, as German philosopher Friedrich Nietzsche said: "Without music, life would be a mistake."

Way back around 500BC, Confucius wrote: "When music and

courtesy are better understood and appreciated, there will be no war."

Closer to home, Jimi Hendrix said: "Music is a safe kind of high."

That's enough procrastinating. Just go and practise!

Here are the tools for

Star Performance!

Books & Workshops
by Ruth Bonetti
enable confident performance

Practice WAS a Dirty Word – Music Journal

A half-hour music lesson = 0.3% of a student's week. Here's how to reinforce the other 99.7%

Ruth Bonetti's innovative PRACTICE DIARY encourages students to take ownership of their time, development and progress, to maximise their talent.

Highlights tips from *Practice is a Dirty Word*

ENJOY music and shine in performance

- Set and reach goals
- Plan practice time
- Problem-solve tricky bars
- Face and master scales
- Revive enthusiasm
- Retain standard in busy times
- Excel in exams and recitals

Confident Music Performance – Fix the Fear of Facing an Audience

You've practised hard, you have ability – but are you able to walk on stage and shine?

This book will help you face the audience without fear, enjoy the moment and succeed.

Shows how to:

- Cure shakes, jitters, brain fog
- Excel in exams, auditions and concerts
- Survive mistakes and hazards on stage
- Enjoy confident performance

For information about Ruth Bonetti's books, to order copies or arrange workshops:

www.ruthbonetti.com
email: ruth@ruthbonetti.com
Ph: (61 7) 3300 2286 or 0411 782 404
Fax: (61 7) 3300 5786

Practice is a Dirty Word – How to Clean up your Act

ISBN: 978-0-9578861-5-5

Practice WAS a Dirty Word – Music Journal

ISBN: 978-0-9578861-2-4

Confident Music Performance – Fix the Fear of Facing an Audience

ISBN: 978-0-9578861-6-2

Don't Freak Out, Speak Out – Public Speaking With Confidence.

This invaluable guide for speakers covers all aspects of preparation – mental, emotional, physical and presentation.
A must for all who stand up and speak in public.

Available also as audio CD and e-book at **www.ruthbonetti.com**

Also by Ruth Bonetti – available at leading music stores:

Enjoy Playing the Clarinet (Oxford University Press) — A comprehensive beginner tutor (listed, AMEB Grades 1-4)

"One of the best tutors for beginners, full of sound teaching ideas, attractive and challenging tunes and clever drawings." – Paul Harvey, *Winds Magazine*

What critics and readers say about Ruth Bonetti's books…

"Ruth Bonetti has inspired me. I'm off to make music."

– Good Reading

"Thank you from the core of my heart for illuminating me with techniques to overcome stage fear. I am very grateful!"

– Sandeep Harish, India

"Stimulating, thought provoking, and engagingly written by an experienced professional musician and music teacher, this is a highly recommended volume for music teachers, parents and music students."

– AccessEd

"Your books are so good they should be bottled!"

– Dr Anna Burrows, The Gap, Australia

"A healing, compassionate little book."

– Margery Smith, Lecturer, University of Newcastle, Australia

"This easy to read, gem of a publication gives lots of practical, down-to-earth advice … written in a sympathetic, user-friendly style, it is highly recommended."

– Dr Rita Crews, The Studio

"This book is a Godsend! Can you imagine never again having to nag your student to practise? This book could be the end of all your woes!"

– Mary Nemet, Strings USA

"It is mandatory reading for all would-be performers, seasoned or otherwise."

– Stringendo

"Thanks to your books and seminars, I feel a lot better about playing in concerts."

– Oboist Leslie Godfrey, New Jersey, USA

"… So helpful and inspiring that I now incorporate its principles into my performing and teaching. This book is truly a needed resource in this day of beta- blockers and high-pressure audition situations. I know of no other book that addresses this issue in such an engaging manner. It is essential equipment for any musician, professional or student."

– Mary Natvig, PhD Associate Professor, Bowling Green State University, Ohio, US

WORKSHOPS / MASTER CLASSES FOR STUDENTS

Include:

- How to Practise for Success
- How to Impress the Examiner – and Excel
- Scales and Arpeggios Demystified
- 7 Easy Habits for Confident Performance
- Prepare for Confident Oral Presentations
- Enjoy Playing the Clarinet

Days of Excellence Program (Choose modules to suit your program)

WORKSHOPS FOR MUSIC TEACHERS

Topics include:

- How to Motivate, Retain and Inspire Students
- Professional Parent-Teacher Communication
- Prepare Students for Confident Performance
- Empower Students to Realise Performance Potential

TALK FOR PARENTS

- Help your Child Excel with Music

From her perspective as an AMEB examiner, educator and mother of three sons, Ruth solves common issues such as:

"How can I enforce boring practice?"
"Should I sit in on lessons?"
"How to ease performance stress?"
"My child has talent but has lost interest! How do I rekindle their enjoyment?"

"Ruth Bonetti was a faculty asset far beyond our expectations. Students responded so positively to her coaching and vibrant personality that we had to expand her workload and schedule additional sessions. I cannot say enough positive about Mrs Bonetti's work as a performance coach."

Dr Victor E. Gebauer, Executive Director, Lutheran Music Program, Minneapolis, USA

"Ruth delighted the participants with her infectious good humour and vibrant personality. Her presentations were a highlight due to Ruth's ability to involve everyone, her enthusiasm and charisma."

Malcolm F. Potter, President, Music Teachers' Association, South Australia

Index

Notes